HELEN COSTANTINO FIORATTI

PLAYING GAMES

Games
and Their Players
from Antiquity
to the Present

℗
Edizioni Polistampa

Project and implementation
Edizioni Polistampa, Florence

Editing
Monica Roman

Front cover: "Une partie d'échecs qui tourne mal."
Regnault de Montauban, roman en prose (1451-1500).
Paris: Bibliothèque de l'Arsenal, Ms-5073 réserve,
tome 2, fol. 35 (Bibliothèque numérique
Gallica: ark:/12148/btv1b550071656).
Back: Board with scenes of pastimes of courtly life.
Italian School, 15th century. Florence:
Museo Nazionale del Bargello.

www.polistampa.com

© 2014 Edizioni Polistampa
Via Livorno, 8/32 - 50142 Firenze
Tel. 055 737871 (15 linee)
info@polistampa.com
ww.leonardolibri.com

ISBN: 978-88-596-1328-2

Table of Contents

⬤ Alfonso X, Two Men Playing Chess
from *Libro de los Juegos*, ca. 1283, 40 x 28 cm.
San Lorenzo de El Escorial, Spain

⬤ Alfonso X, The Game of
Astronomical Tables from *Libro de los
Juegos*, ca. 1283, 40 x 28 cm.
San Lorenzo de El Escorial, Spain

Introduction

Gaming and gambling are at least as old as civilization. Throughout history, the gaming impulse has manifested itself in a number of ways: in the invention and subsequent modification of games of chance and skill; in a long history of gambling debts and shortfalls; in discoveries in probability and mathematics to predict the outcomes of games; and in technical innovations related to the production of games.

Many colloquialisms in our language today reflect the influence of games and the playing of games throughout history. "The game is up" means it's over, to "lay one's cards on the table" signifies to say what one really means, and "one's strong suit" is a particular strength. To "play by the rules" is the moral way (but perhaps also the unimaginative one), while "playing one's cards well" is making good use of opportunities and "no dice" conveys lack of success or impossibility. How did the language of games and gaming become so common? What did gaming and gambling have that was, and is, so compelling to so many people of different countries, eras, and religions through history?

From the first ancient games, to legislation against gambling in the Middle Ages, to the aristocratic gambling cultures of 18th-century France and Italy, gaming has captivated and enthralled the imagination since the beginning of human history. This book is both a short history and a study of different types of games (many of which have endured to the present, and the profound effect that gaming and gambling have had on culture and society) from ancient to modern times.

Alfonso X, Two Men in a Tent (Chess Problem # 89) from *Libro de los Juegos*, ca. 1283, 40 x 28 cm. San Lorenzo de El Escorial, Spain

GAMING AND GAMBLING
THROUGH HISTORY
AND VARIOUS CULTURES

Nicolas Tournier, *Dice Players*, ca. 1619,
oil on canvas, 47 5/16 x 67 1/2 cm.
Speed Art Museum, Louisville,
Kentucky, 1987.12

Early History of Games: Asia, Europe, the Middle East and the Americas

The best cast of dice is to cast them quite away
Henry Smith, *Sermons*, 1585

○ *Game of Hounds and Jackals,* Egypt, ca. 1814-1805 B.C., ivory and ebony, 6.3 x 15.2 cm. The Metropolitan Museum of Art, New York, 26.7.1287a-k

The English word for games derives from the Anglo-Saxon *gamen* meaning sport or play. In Italian, the word for games, or to play, is *giocare* or *giuocare*. To game can mean to take part in a game, to gamble and also to trifle, to deceive, to make a fool of someone. *Giocarsi* means to gamble away, to cheat or deceive. In French, *jeu* or *jeux* means play or game, gambling games are called *jeu d'argent*, and the stakes are *enjeux*. To gamble in German is *spielen* while "game" is *spiel* and *man spielt ein spiel* is 'to play a game'.

Games and gambling are closely entwined, and both are ancient pastimes.

Ancient cultures from China, the Near East, Egypt, India, Greece and Rome, and the Americas have all left evidence of early gaming. Gaming boards from Mesopotamia—precursors to the backgammon board—dating from 5000 years ago have been found in what is now modern Iraq. Gaming also appears in the wall decorations of ancient Egyptian tombs.

Egyptian wall paintings depicting gods and mortals tossing knucklebones (the small bone under a sheep or even a dog's heel) have survived from as early as 3500 B.C.[1] These bones, called *astragals*, were the early equivalent of dice. The same Egyptian wall paintings also show boards that served to record and tally the players' scores, though the rules of those ancient games are now

[1]   Knucklebones evolved into what are now referred to as "jacks" a game using six-pointed metal stars and a rubber ball instead of stones or animal bones. Variations of jacks are played all over the world: it is known as "gobs" in Ireland, "five rocks" in Turkey, and *gongi* in Korea.

unknown. Both adults and children in Ancient Greece and Rome played with astragals. They were usually made of bone but could also be made of stone or metal incised with figural representations. Narrow throwing sticks used for gaming throughout the ancient world are still in use by some Native American and Arab populations. In the Mongol steppe region Genghis Khan is documented as having played knucklebone games with his boyhood friend Jamuka, who would later become his archrival.

According to H.I.A. Murray (1866-1955), board games can be classed into five different types: games where the

Queen Nefertari Playing Senet, facsimile of a wall painting in the Tomb of Nefertari, Egypt, ca. 1279-1213 B.C., tempera on paper, 43 x 46 cm. The Metropolitan Museum of Art, New York, 30.4.145

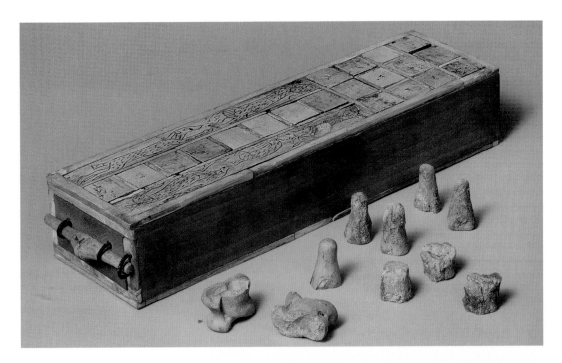

● *Game Box for Playing Senet and Twenty Squares*, Egypt, ca. 1635-1458 B.C., ivory, copper alloy, wood, 25 x 6.7 x 5 cm. The Metropolitan Museum of Art, New York, 16.10.475a

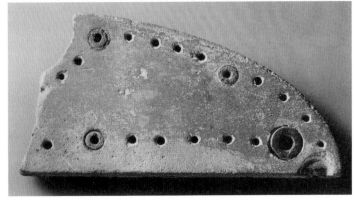

● *Game Board of 58 Holes* from Iran, ca. 2055-1650 B.C.

goal is to get one's pieces in a specific configuration; "war" games that have the aim of capturing and immobilizing the opponent's pieces; "hunt" games in which one player has more pieces and seeks to immobilize an opponent's smaller force; "race" games where the victor is the first to get his pieces to the finish using dice or other lots; and *Mancala* games in which the aim is to capture a majority of neutral pieces.

Board games sometimes relied on dice, lots, or sticks to move pieces along the board. According to Sophocles, Palamedes invented counting and dice during the ten-year siege of Troy to render the time spent there less painfully boring. Dice have been found dating back to 3000 B.C., by which time cubic dice had mostly replaced the earlier long die. Dice dating from ca. 1400 B.C. have been found in present-day Pakistan on the banks of the Indus River with their points arranged as those we know today.[2] The six-faced cube dice numbered with dots adding up to seven on opposite sides became common in Greece from 700 B.C. onwards.

In Sumeria dice were pyramidal, while in Egypt, four-sided dice have been found in Egyptian tombs. Etruscan dice from approximately 900 B.C. were quite similar to modern dice. Gaming sticks found with *Senat* boards in Egypt dating to around 1500 B.C. are similar to those used today in Middle Eastern, Korean, and Native Americans games.

In 1919 a type of race game excavated in Sudan (possibly from Tyre in Lebanon) and dating from the Middle Bronze Age (ca. 2000-1500 B.C.) was a board with ivory pegs of horse and hound heads. This was a popular game played from Egypt to Iran in which pieces, by counts of dice, were moved down one row of holes and up another on their respective sides. The first player to reach the hole at the top probably seized an opposing piece. The game continued until one player won all of the opponent's pieces. The lines connecting the holes may have been shortcuts or forced retreats.

Trays which were possible supports for games have been found dating from the seventh millennium B.C. in the Fertile Crescent, well before complete games were excavated. In Egypt, Senet (or Senat), a kind of race game composed of thirty pieces, was in evidence in the Roman era. A Senet-type game of twenty pieces appeared in Iran and Mesopotamia, probably imported from the Indus Valley and linked to the famous game from Ur that dates to 2600 B.C. The Egyptian game used both sides of a box with Senet on one side and the game of twenty holes on the other. It was undoubtedly sufficient (where game boards have not been found) for the players to trace the game's grill in the earth or sand. At Ephesus and Didyme, games were in fact scratched into the steps of the temples. A configuration game called Dog and the Jackal, related

● *Three Dice* from Pompeii, 1st Century A.D., bone. Musée Condé, Chantilly, France, OA 1865; OA 1866; OA 1867

[2]   Examples of Ancient Roman dice can be seen in the Nazionale Museo delle Marche in Ancona, Italy. Roman dice of amber, ivory, and agate from Pompeii, Herculaneum, and Sicily were among the antiquities Sir William Hamilton, British ambassador to the court of Naples from 1764-1800, sold to recoup some of his costs of representing his country.

to games of thirty points and the game of "58 holes", had a great diffusion from the Nile Valley through Iran and Anatolia (modern western Turkey).

According to Herodotus, writing in the 5th century B.C., gaming was such a diversion that it could even be used to ward off hunger. A popular scene decorating Etruscan mirrors and Greek vases was that of Achilles and Ajax playing a game involving a board divided into zones with two dice or pawns. This game used a sort of chessboard, called a *tabula lusoria*, and a pouch of pawns which would be advanced across the board. An example of another game requiring these multiple pawns—known as *latrunculi* or "little robbers"—was discovered in a tomb in Campania (Italy) and included an entire collection of the carved-bone pieces.

From 200 B.C. to 200 A.D., the Chinese played a popular game called *liuba* in which dice and gaming pieces were used with a marked board. Excavations have uncovered such boards dating from the Han Dynasty (206 B.C.-220 A.D.) In one story, the 8th-century Chinese Emperor Xuanzong, was playing Go (*weiqi*, a strategic game played with black and white counters) with a prince and was about to lose when the Emperor's favorite concubine, Yang Guifei, dropped a tiny dog from Samarkand on the board, scattering all the pieces, and greatly pleasing the Emperor.

The Chinese developed *mahjong*, playing cards, and dominoes. The oldest extant examples of dominoes were found in the tomb of Tutankhamen in Egypt. Four early examples of whale bone dominoes have been found, but the oldest European dominoes date only to the 17th century. Dominoes, or tiles, have twenty-eight pieces numbered from one to six where all the possible combinations must be represented only once and, like playing cards, a variety of games can be played with a set of dominoes.

The origin myth of mahjong is that Confucius developed and popularized the game around 500 B.C. The three dragon tiles were said to represent the three Confucian cardinal virtues, his fondness for birds reflected in the name 'mahjong' (the names of the tiles mean 'cardinal' and 'sparrow' in Chinese). Though there is no evidence that the game existed prior to the 19th century, it may, however, be based on an older Chinese card game variously called *madiao, matiae,* or *yesi.* Mahjong was banned by the People's Republic in 1949, when gambling activities were regarded as symbols of corrupt capitalism. After the Cultural Revolution it grew in popularity in China and elsewhere in Asia. In the 1920s the U.S. company Abercrombie and Fitch introduced mahjong to America after sending agents to Chinese villages to buy as many mahjong sets as they could find, quickly selling twelve-thousand sets. It continued to be extremely popular throughout the 1920s and 1930s in America.

Also in Asia, a popular board game with a coiled snake marked with the moves (sometimes as many as five hundred) along its sides, was called Snakes. It was played with dice substitutes and may have originated around 3000 B.C.

A popular European race game that was widely dispersed, generically called *jeu de l'oie* (Game of the Goose) or *gioco dell'oca* in Italy, has many variations. Legend has it that this game too was played during the long siege of Troy. A 17th-century example of a *jeu de l'oie* was sold in 2001 at the Drouot auction house in Paris called *Jeu du Sphère ou de l'Univers,* made in 1661 by Etienne Vourillemont.[3] The game continues to be re-imagined with different themes and illustrations even today.

● *Liubo Board and Pieces* from Henan Province, 206 B.C.-220 A.D., earthenware with pigment and bone, 36.2 x 31.4 x 5.1 cm., The Metropolitan Museum of Art, New York 1994.285a—m

[3]   Other board games in the same sale included *jeu du blason* (from 1718), *jeu des courses de chevaux* (from 1742), *jeu instructif des fables de La Fontaine* (from 1780), *jeux de pans en miniature* (from 1803), *jeu royal de la vie d'Henri IV* and *jeux de l'oie renouvelés des grecs* from (1815).

Circular Game Board from Egypt, ca. 3100-2686 B.C., limestone, 7 cm x 37 mm x 37 cm. The British Museum, London EA66216

The Middle East was a source of many games now played in the West, such as checkers (draughts), chess, backgammon, and Parcheesi. Parcheesi (or pachisi) was the ultimate chase, race, and capture game and came to central Europe via England. Other race games of the "cross and circle" type such as *ludo* appear throughout Asia.[4] A Korean cross-and-circle game, known in 3rd-century China, was considered the ancestor of such games, although in China the game was considered a lower-class gambling game. Cross-and-circle boards have also been found engraved on stones from the 7th century at Mayan archaeological sites in Central America.

In Mesoamerica evidence of gaming comes from game boards 1200 years old etched into stone or scratched into stucco found near modern Mexico City, and in Copan in Northern Honduras. In the Americas, tracts of land could be used as game boards. 5000 years ago, in the center of an island swamp in Southern Mexico (Tiac Chiapas), Mexicans built superimposed clay floors with smooth surfaces that made harvesting clam shells, used for gaming, convenient. The floors reveal oval patterns used as boards for "race and war" games. The object of the "war" game was to capture an opponents' pieces, and in the race games the winner was the first to reach a finish. The boards could be improvised with arrangements of small stones, or, if stones were unavailable, by digging small holes.

[4] Game sets from the 12th to the 19th century were displayed in 2005 at the Sackler Gallery in Washington, D.C. Also shown were 16th to 18th century Persian and Indian illuminated manuscripts and paintings featuring games.

● Aztec game of patolli

Modern Mayans still play a war dice game called Bul using maize kernels to celebrate the start of the planting season. In the ancient Aztec capital of Tenochtitlán?, a popular game described by Spanish friars in the 16th century was played with split reed dice, a game board pressed into the stucco floor (resembling a lottery board), with pebbles as game pieces. The Mayans also reportedly wagered on ball games where the losing team's captain could be sacrificed. Let us hope these were just tales!

Spanish priests described Aztec versions of checkers, dice games, and bowling which allowed players from different areas to come together for days to feast and gamble, perhaps as a means to distribute wealth. Gamblers invoked the god Macuilxochitl for luck and heavy betting by players and onlookers was reported; one gambling addict wagered everything he had playing *patolli* and *lachil*, two types of ball games.[5] Not being able to pay gambling debts could have fatal consequences: it was punishable by hanging.

It is clear that games and gambling have always been closely allied. The roots of gambling date from prehistory where sticks, bones, pebbles and shells, could be tossed, rolled, drawn or thrown. The casting of objects, or lots, had religious connotations which were thought to divine or predict the future. Over time, casting lots evolved into wagers simply for gain. In Greek mythology, the three brothers Zeus, Poseidon, and Hades drew lots to decide who would rule the world. Zeus won, becoming lord of

5   Barbara Voorhies, "Games and Other Amusements of the Ancient Mesoamericans", http://www.mexicolore.co.uk/aztecs/home/games-and-other-amusements-of-the-ancient-mesoamericans, 24/01/2014

the skies and king of the Gods, Poseidon was made sovereign of the seas, while Hades was relegated to the underworld to preside over the dead. This must be the description of the biggest gamble of all time!

The Greeks bet on the outcome of the Olympic Games and played heads or tails with painted shells. The Romans wagered on gladiatorial combats and chariot races. In the *popinae*, eating houses which were described in many writings as immoral places, Romans could eat and drink and lay bets or *sponsiones*. Since political debates also took place in the *popinae*, imperial restrictions were enacted against gambling there.

In China gambling houses appeared about 2000 B.C. Asian folktales tell of gamblers wagering their families and even offering their own bodies (and their body parts) as stakes. According to the 1st-century B.C. Hindu epic, *The Mahabharata*, the world was conceived as a game of chance. In another Indian legend, the *Rigveda*, the god Savit implored people to plow their furrows and not waste time playing with dice. This injunction would be repeated often throughout history.

Sometimes gambling did not even require dice, lots, or game boards. In Ancient Greece and Rome, for example, *morra*, or *marelle*, now known as Rock, Paper, Scissors, was played. In this game one used fingers to play, sometimes for fun, but it could also be used to determine more seri-

Syrian game

ous questions. With only two players (it was possible to have more), each threw out a single hand showing from zero to five fingers while calling out a guess of the sum. The correct guess won a point and the first player to receive five points won the game. One version of morra, *micatio*, was played in southern Italy; with four-person teams competing one at a time, and a total of four turns per team member, the match was won with eleven points. The game called *micare digitis*, or "to flash with the fingers", led to a Roman saying, "he is a worthy man with whom you could play micatio in the dark", meaning that the man in question was honest and trustworthy. Micatio settled disputes over the sale of merchandise in the Roman Forum until Apronius, the prefect of Rome, banned it. In Arab countries micatio is called *mukharaja*, in France *la main chaude*, and in China and Mongolia *hua quan*, or "fist quarrel".

Another ancient game that needed neither board nor dice is still played in the Molise region of Italy. In the "egg war", each player has five eggs, the first player holds the egg in his fist on the playing surface, while the second player holds the egg similarly and uses it as a hammer to attack the adversary's egg (only cracking it so the egg could still be eaten). The winner of the game is the one with the last unbroken egg in hand. The prize is possession of all the cracked eggs, thus assuring even the poorest a holiday meal for his family.[6]

The Roman Emperor Augustus (27 B.C.) liked to gamble in his leisure hours. Surviving letters by Augustus to his stepson Tiberius tell of one occasion in which he and another relative, Drusus, spent all day gambling during a public holiday. The emperor showed himself to be a good loser, which was noted as an unusual quality in a ruler.[7]

In the 1st century A.D., the Emperor Claudius played dice frequently. For the populace, however, play was forbidden except at special times, suggesting that gambling was already considered a problem. The Greek historian Polybius described Roman soldiers playing at draughts (checkers) on top of a famous picture by Aristeides (Strabo VIII.6.28).

Even though Plutarch described Marcus Porcius Cato as dour, he made exceptions for alcohol and gambling,

[6]   It was traditionally played the Saturday before Easter, but it is now played all year in the Roccarainola area. This "egg war" is also played around Easter in the United States using traditional, dyed, hard-boiled eggs.
[7]   Anthony Everitt, *Augustus: The Life of Rome's First Emperor* (New York: Random House, 2006), p. 264.

which he endorsed. The great orator Cicero thought that Mark Antony was an unreliable drunk, a political gambler (*aleator*), and "dice-thrower". Cicero also accused the debt-ridden aristocrat Catiline of seeking support for revolution in 62 A.D. from those who wasted their ancestral fortunes on sex, gluttony, and gambling, during a time when gambling was illegal in Rome.

During the launch of the civil war Julius Caesar ordered his loyal soldiers to invasion with the cry of, "Let the dice fly high!" as if he were playing a game of chance. According to Suetonius, Caesar, when crossing the Rubicon with his army, said, "*alea iacta est*", or the "die is cast", meaning there would be no going back. He was also said to have used the phrase, "it's dicey", meaning the outcome was unpredictable.

Mark Antony played games with Caesar's nephew Octavian, his adopted heir. The rivals also bet on cockfights, played cards, and cast lots to decide political matters, but, according to Suetonius' 2nd-century *The Lives of the Caesars*, Mark Antony usually lost. According to Plutarch, Mark Antony also played dice and drank with Cleopatra. In his 1st-century A.D. *Germania*, Tacitus wrote of the northern barbarians' love of drinking and addiction to gambling.

Games provided not only a distraction, but metaphors for medieval Muslim theologians: the debate over predestination versus free will was symbolically represented in games like backgammon and chess.

Among "sowing" games, a very early game excavated in what is today northern Israel belongs to a family of board games called "count and capture" games. The games are still played in Asian and African countries, comparable to

● Possibly Bullom. *Mancala Game Board*, 19th Century, wood, 21 x 59.1 x 13 cm. Brooklyn Museum, 22.239

chess in the West. A gaming board from ca. 1300 A.D. was discovered in the ancient city of Megidda in the Jezreel Valley. The ivory oval board with an ivory ring at the top was for the game of 58 holes, with holes to put pegs into and every fifth hole inlaid with gold.[8]

Mancala (sowing games) comes from the Arabic *nagala* meaning "to move". Mancala appears in Egypt, Lebanon and Syria in various versions, one known as the game *kalah*. The game is thought to have originated in Ethiopia and Madagascar, where the results of games were also consulted for political decisions and used for divination. Mancala is a sequence of picking up seeds (beans, pebbles and peanuts were also used) from a hole, then "sowing" them, eventually capturing all the opponent's seeds based on the state of the board. The boards, which sometimes folded, could be made of various materials with a series of holes arranged in rows, usually two or four.[9] They include depressions called "pits" or "houses". The large holes at the end of some boards were used for holding captured pieces. The game emerged from agriculturally-based societies and may be older than its documented 1300 years.

⬤ Jean-Baptiste Greuze, *A Game of Morra*, ca. 1756, ink, wash, graphite, 25 x 36 cm. Morgan Library and Museum, New York

[8] Now in the Oriental Institute Museum of the University of Chicago. The astonishing collection of early game-related objects in this museum includes ancient artifacts from an archeological dig in China under the auspices of the Rockefellers.
[9] Their designs vary, including one called *Endodoi* which has boards measuring 2" x 6" to 2" x 9 7/8" (5 x 15 cm to 5 x 25.5 cm).

The Kurna temple graffiti in Egypt were linked to mancala, but may also be associated with games common to the Roman world. Mancala was popular in Africa, the Caribbean, and Asia, in particular Manchuria.

Mancala was still played in 1895 when Madagascar was invaded by the French. Queen Ranavalona III placed the destiny of the island on the outcome of a game to determine her military strategy. The strategy was ruinous and Queen Ranavalona was forced to flee into exile. Merchants in early 17th-century England also played mancala, as did the populations of the Baltic area and territories, modern Turkey, Serbia, and Bosnia (where it was called *ban-ban*). It is still played in many places including the United States, notably in Louisiana. Displayed in the 2007 exhibition *Venice & the Islamic World* at the Metropolitan Museum of Art in New York, Giovanni Antonio Guardi's *Two Odalisques Playing Mancala in the Harem* represents two female players of mancala in a luxurious setting.

An important source concerning the intersection of Per-

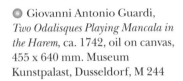 Giovanni Antonio Guardi, *Two Odalisques Playing Mancala in the Harem*, ca. 1742, oil on canvas, 455 x 640 mm. Museum Kunstpalast, Dusseldorf, M 244

sian and European game culture is the *Libro de los Juegos* (*The Book of Games*) commissioned by Alfonso X, King of Leon and Castile, in the 13th century. It was produced by the Dominican friar Jacques de Cessoles of Reims and is now housed in the library of San Lorenzo de El Escorial. The first section of the *Libro de los Juegos* deals with chess, the second with dice games, and the third with miscellaneous games. The book proclaimed to be written for "all those who are looking for a pleasant pastime which will bring them comfort and dispel their boredom".

The *Libro de los Juegos* is illustrated with a series of examples taken from the game of chess, "since every group and every man on the chessboard, as in life, took his place and moved according to fixed rules". The eight chess figures were represented by eight figures, every figure was depicted with a tool and performing a particular task. Only the queen did not work; she was motionless and beautiful.

Gaming and Gambling in Europe: a short history

Dove non corre la moneta, ogn'uom si straca.
Giovanni Maria Cecchi, 16th century[10]

Tacitus, in his *Germania*, wrote critically of the gambling fever of the "German" tribe. Considered less civilized than the Celts (who came from north and east of Gaul), he wrote,

> They practice dice play at which one will naturally wonder, soberly, and quite as if it were serious business, with such hardihood in winning and losing, that, when they have nothing more left, they stake their freedom and their person on the last cast of the dice. The loser resigns himself voluntarily to servitude, and even if he is younger and stronger than his adversary, he allows himself to be bound and sold. Thus great is their staunchness in an affair so bad, they themselves call it 'keeping their word'.[11]

Saint Augustine's condemnation of gaming in ca. 395 A.D. found many echoes throughout the Middle Ages. To him the culprit was clear: "the devil invented dicing".[12] The notoriously dissolute 10th century Pope, John XII, elevated to the Papacy at age 16 in 955, the illegitimate son of his predecessor, called upon pagan gods and goddesses to grant him luck when rolling the dice.

It was already considered a bad practice in England by the 12th century, according to John of Salisbury it was "the mother of lies and perjuries.[13] Frederick II Hohenstaufen, the future Holy Roman Emperor and King of Sicily, reigned over a vast territory when he issued an edict in 1232 against the playing of dice. A similar command was made by Louis IX of France in 1255, due, it was said, to the drinking, idleness, and cheating that were accompaniments to gambling. In Venice, *il Maggior Consiglio* (the

[10] "Where money is not involved, every man becomes bored". Giovanni Maria Cecchi is a 16th-century Tuscan author.
[11] Cited by R.C. Bell, *Board and Table Games from Many Civilizations* (Vol. 1-2, 2012), p. 125.
[12] *Aleam invenit Daemon* (*De civitate dei* lib. 4).
[13] *Mendaciorum et periuriarum mater est alea* (*Policraticus*, Book 1, Chapter 5).

Major Legislative Council) forbade gambling as early as 1254, and again in 1255, 1266, and 1268. Moreover, on March 5, 1296 a Venetian law established that any resident who gambled where wine was sold would be fined one hundred *soldi*, and the accuser would receive one third of the fine. A great incentive!

In the 13th century, games were classified into two groups: those permitted by the Church and those which were not. The Justinian code specified that illicit games were those that involved betting with money. They tolerated modest bets, however, in athletic competition. St. Thomas Aquinas condemned the moral conduct that was often revealed in games: he disapproved of the verbal abuse and blasphemy committed during the heat of play. He considered players diabolical and superstitious and regarded their practice of kissing the dice before throwing them a bad sign.[14] It was an attitude shared by Gabriele of Barletta, a 15th-century Dominican who claimed that "just as God invented the twenty-one letters of the alphabet, the Devil invented dice where there he placed twenty-one points".

In the festive atmosphere which prevailed in the first half of the 13th century at the hot springs in Bagno di Petriolo, Tuscany, a *signore dei bagni* was elected to organize games and entertainments. While gambling was not permitted, chess and checkers were. Since typical cures for skin troubles lasted four to five days (twenty days for other maladies) there was ample time for these pursuits.

In one medieval cautionary tale a young Florentine was attracted to the play of gamblers and proceeded to lose all the money he was carrying belonging to his employer, a wool merchant. The young man went to a usurer and lost all the borrowed money too. He then pledged the clothes he was wearing to the money lender. Since the story was recounted as of particular interest, he must have been reduced to nakedness.[15]

In the early Renaissance, Saint Bernardino of Siena inveighed against gambling in his sermons: he sent terrifying invectives against game playing, saying that it was anti-Christian, created by Lucifer himself, and that the rituals of the game were a reversal of liturgy in glorifying sin. One such sermon entitled *Charticelles seu Naibos* (*A Paper on*

[14] Gabriele of Barletta wrote: "*Sicut Deus invenit XXI literas alphabeti- ita Diabolus invenit dados ubi posuit XXI puncta.*
[15] Giovanni Sercambi, *Novelle: Scrittori d'Italia*, edited by Giovanni Sinicropi, 1972, vol. XXXIIII, p. 159.

● Alfonso X, Four Men Playing at "the World" Backgammon from the *Libro de los Juegos*, ca. 1283. San Lorenzo de El Escorial, Spain

the Game Naibus) was delivered in Bologna where gambling was extremely popular.

In a vain attempt to appease a vengeful God and save themselves from the Black Plague, Sienese officials banned gambling on June 13, 1348. The pestilence reached Siena via Florence, eventually eliminating between 50 and 60 percent of the population, but the ban on gambling was revoked six months later.[16]

In the early 14th century it was reported that Saint Antoninus, archbishop of Florence, disapproved of gaming to such an extent that he overturned a games table in his fury.

The Florentine nobility gambled constantly: in 1433, a group of Florentine patricians were surprised by the

16   John Kelly, *The Great Mortality: An Intimate History of the Black Death* (New York: Harper Perennial, 2006), pp. 117-119.

authorities while gambling at a barber shop on the Ponte Vecchio. Florentines also placed bets on anything. Puccio Pucci placed a bet with a *speziale* (apothecary) named Matteo on the number of fetuses that Matteo's wife was carrying. Matteo declared it was five. He must have been a knowledgeable apothecary because she delivered quintuplets. Pucci did not specify whether the infants or their mother survived, only that he had to pay the seven lire to the *speziale*. Once when asked by a petitioner to pass a law prohibiting priests from gambling in the hopes of improving the city's dismal morals, Cosimo de' Medici, founder of the great dynasty, answered, "first stop them from using loaded dice".[17] In Baldassare Castiglione's 1528 treatise *The Courtier*, the courtiers turn to practical games and parlor games when they are bored. A speaker in the dialogue describes courts where nobles throw food at one another or make bets about eating the most revolting things.

Gaming was clearly counter to medieval notions of chivalry and courtly behavior. Geoffrey de Charney, a highly respected knight who served the 14th-century King Jean of France as standard-bearer, protested against it in his *Livre de Chevalerie* which outlined standards of conduct, piety, and virtue. He disapproved of dice when played for greed, since it "frequently caused the players to suffer great losses".[18] De Charney also castigated the newly popular game of *jeu de paume* (an ancestor of tennis), which made men "lose their goods and inheritance; he instead suggested that knights should joust, talk, dance, and sing decorous songs in the company of ladies".[19] A 1489 woodblock illustration attributed to Albrecht Durer condemns gambling even more strongly with the inscription "all the players of the world are the sons of Satan".

In Switzerland, an ordinance at St. Gallen from 1364 had already forbidden dice games but permitted board games. Card games were soon generally prohibited beginning in 1379. During the period of the Domenican friar Savanarola's influence in Florence, Duke Ercole I of Ferarra on Easter Day April 3, 1496, published a proclamation prohibiting games (lumped together with blasphemy, sodomy, and concubinage).

Medieval and Renaissance Italy saw a different kind of social activity outside the usual family or neighborly gath-

[17] Miles J. Unger, *Magnifico: The Brilliant Life and Violent Times of Lorenzo de' Medici* (New York: Simon & Schuster, 2009), p. 5.
[18] Geoffrey de Charney, *Le livre de Chevalerie Froissart*, Part 3, ca. 1350, pp. 463-533.
[19] De Charney, *Ibid.*, pp. 463-533.

erings. Games of chance (*ad zardum*), especially dice, were what brought men together. In the 14th and 15th centuries, men gambled by day, but even more in private homes by night. Fairs and markets tolerated gambling, but most play outdoors was furtive, taking place in doorways, loggias, alleys, and deserted marketplaces where a candle and muffled voices could go unobserved. These games of chance, especially dice, brought men together from all parts of town.

While writing *The Prince*, Machiavelli wrote to a friend, "after dinner over I go back to the inn. There I generally find the host, a butcher, a miller, and a couple of kiln workers. I mix with these boors the whole day, playing at *cricca* and at *tric trac*, which games give rise to a thousand quarrels and much exchange of bad language, and we generally wrangle over farthings, and our shouting can be heard at San Casciano".[20]

Gaming was so deeply a part of everyday life in Renaissance Italy that it was omnipresent in conversation. In Machiavelli's play *Mandragola*, Frate Timoteo wants to be sure that "this is real money and not gaming counters". In another comedy by Pietro Ariosto, *Il Marescalco* (the table master), the jeweler remarks that the Duke of Mantua "wants to gamble with me today. I'm all set to win a fortune".

Appointed as government representative, the 15th-century magistrate and tax collector of Pescia and Pistoia, Piero de' Pazzi, the son of the distinguished merchant Andrea de' Pazzi, controlled gambling in his capacity as provincial governor but refused (a scruple which was noted as unusual) presents and bribes. In late 15th-century Florence, an anonymous contemporary wrote that Jacopo Pazzi's gambling was one of the roots of the Pazzi rebellion. With the collaboration of Pope Sixtus IV and others, the Pazzis hatched an anti-Medici plot in April 1478 which brought about the ruin of the Pazzi family.[21]

Among the English aristocracy chronic gambling losses appear to have been common. Princess Mary, the daughter of King Edward I, though a nun, traveled with a cavalcade of pages, messengers, and minstrels, along with her ladies and other damsels. One time she lost so heavily gambling at dice that she had to borrow from one of her servants. Considered far worse was the Earl of March

[20] Cricca was a game of cards and trictrac a game of dice. This passage comes from a letter where Machiavelli describes rural life in exile; San Casciano is 16 km from Florence.
[21] They succeeded in murdering Lorenzo the Magnificent's younger brother, Guiliano, but failed to kill Lorenzo.

(later King Edward IV) said to have lost 157 marks on forty-five occasions at a host of games, including ten marks lost betting on cock-fighting on Shrove Tuesday!

The English king's chamberlain had authority to deal with disciplinary matters regarding gambling. Thus, in 1468 the steward, treasurer, and controller of the Duke of Clarence was told to restrain the duke's servants if they were found playing cards, dice, and other games of chance (prohibited except during the twelve days of Christmas). The first offense resulted in the loss of a month's wages. The second offence warranted a month's imprisonment, and the third dismissal.[22]

King Henry VII lost half a mark at cards to his son, the seven-year-old future King Henry VIII on May 23, 1498. The fact that such events were described indicates their significance. Among the games played in England were chess, backgammon, raffle, dice, and cards, as well as a ball game similar to tennis called palm. Henry VIII placed bets, but he, too, made gambling houses illegal. Gaming houses became the center of gaming and social activity after public areas were prohibited, evolving into the private clubs still popular today. The English bet on everything, from games, sporting contests, births, deaths, dogfights and any conceivable object. Oliver Cromwell tried to curtail gaming but failed, adding fuel to the general reaction against the government's repression of gambling.

Queen Elizabeth I's relative, the Earl of Kent, inherited his titles and lands in 1503, while he was in his late twenties. His father's deathbed prediction was that his son "not thrive, but be a waster." In fact, young Kent squandered prodigious amounts of money at the gaming tables of the inns of Lombard near his London house.

A haunt for gamblers at the sign of the GEORGE, brokers and Italian money lenders were all ready to extend Kent credit. Finally, he was undone by his great debts, which he thought were taken over by King Henry VII, to save him from his creditors. But the crown in fact then tricked him out of his properties.

Mary and her sister Anne Boleyn, future queen of Henry VIII, played cards and "tables" (backgammon) regularly together after six o'clock supper at their childhood home, Hever Castle. In November 1530 King Henry VIII

● Manuscript of King Alfonso X, Game of pelota.
Las Cantigas de Santa Maria, XII century, San Lorenzo de El Escorial

22 Quoted in William Manchester, *The World Lit Only by Fire: The Medieval Mind and the Renaissance, Portrait of an Age* (New York: Little, Brown and Company, 1992).

gave Anne Boleyn 20 pounds (the equivalent of approximately 6,500 English pounds today) to redeem a jewel from her sister Mary. Either it was one he had given Mary during their affair or, more likely, Mary had won it from him by gambling.

Eleonora of Toledo, the daughter of the Spanish Viceroy of Naples, married Cosimo I de' Medici, the first Grand Duke of Tuscany, in 1539. She received a monetary settlement when she married and was an asset to the Medici for dynastic and political reasons. Eleonora did business, performed charity work, and founded churches, but her real passion was gambling. Card games, dice games, memory games, and games to test general knowledge were popular at the Medici court at the villa of Eleonora and Cosimo's daughter, Isabella de' Medici. Here men and women played against each other and a frequent complaint at the Italian courts was that the males allowed the women to win, which did not make for real competition. In 1561 Girolomo Bargali of Siena compiled *The Dialogue of Games* for Isabella with the aim of promoting interaction amongst the players. A popular game was Of the Ear (known as 'telephone' today), in which each player recited a line of verse beginning with the next letter of the alphabet. Other games, which encouraged teasing and flirting, included one called Devil's Music, and the imitation of animal sounds. The games Portraits of Beauty and Painting required men to extol the physical (and spiritual) beauty of the women using the language of Petrarch and Ariosto. The game of Misfortune required a player to recount an amorous misfortune where a judge would find the lover at fault or innocent. For the game of Slaves and of Servants, men and women players would be "sold" into service to the highest bidder, while the game of Madness had those declared maddened by unrequited love "locked up" in an asylum. In another game, The School Master, players taking silly names would be "instructed" by another player in the role of teacher. They could also pretend to be nuns and monks and enact religious ceremonies—rather blasphemous!

In a 15th-century dialogue written by the architect Leon Battista Alberti, in his four *Libri della Famiglia*, his character Leonardo states, "Any game played sitting down is [not] proper to a really virile man. Perhaps some such games should be allowed the old, chess and similar pleasures for the gouty, but no game that doesn't require exercise and effort seems to me permissible to young and robust boys. Our young men should also make use of the ball. It is an ancient sport and highly suited to produce the agility which is praised in a noble person".

In 1565 gaming was forbidden in the taverns of Florence and the result was that street corners became noisy and congested with players. The next year another law was passed, this time prohibiting gaming on any street or square, although it was permitted along the walls encircling the city. If anyone was found playing within the city he could be given twenty-five lashes. By 1590 cards and dice were prohibited in any public place, including along the river Arno and then even along the city's outer walls. Spectators could also be punished.

Playing dice was outlawed on Tuscan ships. Table games that required dice were allowed if the prize was not monetary but food which had to be consumed immediately. In 1606, players were condemned to the galleys for playing, but by 1681, when fewer people were needed to row the galleys, they could get away with a fine of 100 *scudi*. To discourage players' recourse to usury, lenders could be fined and arrested if it became known a loan was needed for gambling debts.

Despite the so-called immorality of gambling, Florence benefited from a lottery to alleviate financial troubles. Considerable money, which was looked upon as a "voluntary" tribute from the public, was raised with lotteries. Clandestine lotteries, however, at the port of Leghorn were targeted by the police, as were the many maritime gambling activities of the seamen.

The French card game, *bassette*, was forbidden in Florence and then outlawed in all of Tuscany. The fine for transgressors was initially set at two hundred *scudi* and by 1698 the fine had grown to three hundred *scudi*.[23] People paid little attention to these laws. The police were not actually allowed in places where nobles gathered, so the nobles played undisturbed. Despite anti-gambling laws, Florentines bet on everything: the outcome of sieges, the elevation of cardinals, horse races, the elections or death of a pope, and on commerce in general. Pregnant women

[23] During the late 1600's a skilled artisan would earn 50-60 *scudi* per year.

● Girl with bat and ball, 15th
Century, fresco. Castello
Borromeo, Milan

actually set up counters to take bets as to the gender of their expected baby (*maschio e femmina*), which allowed them to put some money aside. This lasted until 1550 when the bets became the responsibility of the husband or father-in-law. One method used to calculate odds was the addition of the wife's and the husband's names (each letter of the alphabet was assigned a number), and, if the total was an even number, the child would be a girl, if the total was odd, a boy would be born. Very scientific! Betting on ships' arrivals, departures and the outcome of voyages was the beginning of what would become the insurance business. Tuscan edicts against such betting were issued in 1569, 1578, and 1587.

Venice was notorious for gambling. The ruling *Consiglio dei Dieci* continually tried to suppress games of chance from the 13th through 18th centuries. A law against betting was issued on March 26, 1506 and then in 1522 a decree was issued in Venice by the Council of Ten clearly stating that:

> Under no circumstances will we tolerate this new game that has begun for some days to take money from him or her which is called Lotto, with such universal murmurings on the destruction of all its participants as well as because of the inconveniences and disorders that come from these so that it is necessary to take provisions against it. On the authority of this council tomorrow morning we will publish on the steps of the Rialto and in San Marco an edict declaring that no one may start another lottery in our city on pain of two years in our prisons and a 500 ducat fine . . . And from this day and for all of March during Carnival . . . you cannot pull on or take out any tickets according to the said penalty.[24]

The diarist Marino Sanudo noted that this attempt was generally ignored and that the Rialto remained full of lotteries despite the threat to confiscate the prizes. Eventually the Council of Ten had a change of heart, and the scheme was deemed suitable for public purposes. To control this new form of salesmanship, the Venetian government sent observers to witness the drawing of lots and soon began using it to raise funds for its own govermentpurposes.[25]

[24]   Marino Sanudo, *I diari di Marino Sanudo*, edited by Rinaldo Fulin (Charleston, S.C.: Nabu Press, 1903), pp. 204-5.
[25]   Sanudo, *Ibid.*, p. 205.

Visitors to Venice in the early 16th century docked at what Petrarch called San Marco's Marble Shore. The travelers were greeted there by pimps and card sharks waiting at the gambling tables along with the requisite tour guides. The famous gigantic venetian map by Jacobo de' Barbari of 1500 (now in the Correr Museum of Venice) pictures the lagoon side of the old mint with the gambling tables and food stalls between the great granite columns facing the harbor.

On December 4, 1621 several Venetian gaming culprits were sentenced as follows: "yesterday morning three lashes were given to the three found playing at Santa Maria Nuovo. The other seven were condemned to time in prison in the dark".[26] In Venice, games were divided into three categories: games of luck, mixed games or those of commerce, and games of ability or industry.[27]

Regarding the Italians' gambling habits during the Renaissance, the 19th-century German scholar Jacob Burckhardt wrote:

> In Italy, the passion for play reached an intensity which often threatened or altogether broke up the existence of the gambler. Florence had found already, at the end of the fourteenth century, its Casanova, a certain Buonaccorso Pitti who in the course of his incessant journeys as a merchant, political agent, diplomat, and professional gambler, won and lost sums so enormous that none but princes like the Dukes of Brabant and Savoy were able to compete with him. That great lottery bank, which was called the Court of Rome, accustomed people to a need of excitement which found its satisfactions in games of hazard during the intervals between one intrigue and another. We read, for example, how Franceschetto Cibo, in two games with Cardinal Raffaello Riario, lost no less than fourteen thousand ducats, and afterwards complained to the Pope that his opponent had cheated him. Italy has, since that time, been the home of the lottery.[28]

Gambling was rampant in Papal Rome too. A twenty-five-year veteran of the Papal state service, Alessandro Pallantieri landed in jail at least twice, and in his writings, he tried to pass off his wealth (derived from graft and other

---

[26]   Beltrami. *Storia della popolazione de Venezia dalla fine del secolo XVI alla caduta della Repubblica* (Padua: Cedam, 1954).
[27]   M.A. Savelli, *Pratica Universale* (1707).
[28]   Jacob Burckhardt, *The Civilization of the Renaissance in Italy* (London: G. Allen & Unwin, 1921), p. 436.

unfair practices) as being due to his skill and luck in gambling. He described the context of his gambling at the Vatican in the following text:

> And since, at the time of Pope Julius II, both His Holiness and the cardinals and the bishops and all the court gambled, I was caught up in the dance too, gambling with the others, and His Holiness sent for me almost every day to have me come and play. And among the other times, when I went to the villa of His Holiness to bring complaint of certain things that Signor Ascanio Colonna was doing to keep provisions from coming to Rome, His Holiness said nothing to me about this except, "Make yourself welcome! Just now, we were missing a fourth player!" And when I told him that His Holiness had laid on my shoulders the burden of the Grain Office and that there was need to attend to other things than playing, His Holiness replied, "I am amazed at you! Is there lack of grain in Campo di Fiori? Stay here to eat. And eat with Michelangelo, and order something good!" And another time, when he had me called to the palace to gamble, I told him, "Holy Father, I have things to do. I have won some *scudi*. I wouldn't like to lose them". His Holiness said, "You have to play. If you lose, it does not matter. I will show you how! Find something to steal for you and for me!" So I played many times both with His Holiness, and in his presence, with his brother, Signor Baldovino. After the midday meal, it was the only thing they did, and I was almost always among the invited . . . [a]nd when I went to a banquet, when I played with His Excellency [Del Monte] and with cardinals and other prelates, it was my good luck that in the house of Monsignor Pavia, who was governor, I won several thousand *scudi*, as all Rome knows.[29]

In 1588 a Roman law stated that, "ancient experience demonstrates how pernicious gaming is. It gives rise to loss of private wealth and ruin to entire families".[30] The law was issued by the Ufficio dei Sensali delle Scomesse, which also provided licenses for betting on the sex of unborn children. During the 17th century the Papal States derived revenue by taxing and fining card games and dicing, though officially these were censured; however, board games were excluded from the edict. To take the place of the prohibited pastimes, penalties and reward games were

[29] Thomas V. Cohen, *Love and Death in Renaissance Italy* (Chicago: University of Chicago Press, 2004), p. 134.
[30] Quoted in John Dickie, *Delizia!* (London: Hodder & Stoughton, 2007).

played with the throw of dice. Money could still be lost or won with the games and some had forfeits or prizes.

In the 17th century, Cardinal Mazarin, the Italian-born prime minister of France, sent his ambassador, Grenouille, to seek a favor of Pope Innocent X. He instructed Grenouille to lose at cards with Donna Olimpia, the sister-in-law of, and power behind, the Pope. The ambassador from Lucca had already observed that Olimpia's Pamphili palazzo was the site of frequent gambling. A refined way of bribing Olimpia to intervene with the Pope was to lose vast sums to her at the games table: "a great expression of affection and desire to earn Grenouille's approval, declaring herself his special servant, exaggerating that there would never be an occasion when she would not do her best to serve him was the result of her winning so royally. Sometimes those desirous of losing to Olimpia failed and the "unfortunates" won despite their best efforts, knowing they would never get anywhere with the Pope from then on.[31]

Economical ruin by means of gambling was not just a urban problem, it affected the French provinces as well. In 1769, an anonymous letter denounced the *brelan* and *lansquenet* tables that attracted the young bourgeoisie and craftsmen and their money:

> It is shameful for an honest man to write an anonymous letter, but I am forced to do so in spite of myself for fear that otherwise some harm might befall me. As a father I am pleased to beg you to put an end to a game of chance that has long existed in our town. My children are ruining me, to say nothing of the other families that have also been ruined. The guilty party is Sieur Balada, a stranger to these parts, who was driven out of Pamiers for having operated a card game there. He has a house near the Franciscans which is used only for gambling. I know that Mondrien (the first consul) warned him not to operate this game, but in spite of that he continues to do so night and day. This is a scandalous thing near a church from which they can be heard shouting and fighting.

Those who operated gambling dens were often accused of inducing their habitués to commit robbery to cover their considerable losses.

[31] Donata Chiomenti Vassalli, *Donna Olimpia o del nepotismo nel Seicento* (Milan: Mursia 1979).

ORO COPERTO NON SI PAGA

● *Lotto Board Game* from Venice, mid-18th Century, painted canvas. Private Collection

By the 18th century, the outcome of pregnancies and the Pope's health were of less interest than betting on horse races and other gaming pursuits. In 1773 the government of Tuscany prohibited card playing in public places, so the cafés turned to billiards. Clerics in Tuscany in the 17th and 18th centuries, however, did not consider gambling a mortal sin unless played with malice.[32]

In Russia, the aristocracy gambled frequently as well. In 1744 the German princess Sophie of Anhalt Zerbst (the young Catherine the Great) accompanied by her mother arrived in Moscow to marry Peter, the heir to the Russian throne. She was met by the nobility, and there followed "endless games of cards with which the court passed the time between Lenten Vigil services".[33] When the engaged couple visiting the Razumovsky estate were joined by the Empress Elizabeth, they gambled for a fortnight.[34]

In the 18th century, William Byrd III of Virginia, while visiting England, lost thousands of pounds gaming, which

[32] … *onde è che da peccato grave colpì quei chierici, i quali vadano in abito non talare, che giuochino a dadi, che giuochiono alle carte, e che attendano in fino a mercatore.* "Whence it is that [it] exonerated those clerics of grave sin, the clerics who go forth not in a priest's cassock, who play dice, who play cards and stay until the end of the market" (P. Segneri, *Lettera su la materia del Probabile* 1703).
[33] Simon Dixon, *Catherine the Great* (New York: Ecco, 2010), p. 49.
[34] *Ibid.*, p. 53.

is said to have motivated his suicide. In late 17th-century America, however, few people had either the leisure or resources for gambling. But by the 18th century gaming and gambling had established itself in almost every social sphere. Card games in Colonial America could begin after supper and continue until dawn. Dicing was a common pastime and bets were made on cockfights, dogs killing rats, and wrestling matches. The most popular wager of all was to bet on horse racing. When the Hempstead Plain in Long Island seemed too inconvenient for New York City bettors, a track was built in Manhattan.

During the 1770s many race tracks were founded in the American South. George Washington himself was a member of the Alexandria Jockey Club and a club in Annapolis. Public roads could also be used for impromptu horse races. In 1776, the Grand Jury in Philadelphia warned of the dangers of horse-racing in the streets because the city had grown in population.

Gambling occurred regularly in the Continental and British armies during the Revolutionary War. Washington issued a directive in 1776 against wagering and forbidding the playing of cards or other games of chance: "At this time of public distress men may find enough to do in the service of their God and their country, without abandoning themselves to vice and immortality". Starving soldiers at Valley Forge even rolled dice to win acorns to eat. The British army had the same problems. When the French appeared toward the end of the war, they invented a form of whist they called Boston; when this game arrived in St. Louis, it became a popular pastime.

In the 1820s and 1830s in America, the social acceptance of gaming declined in response to a religious revival. This did not really have an impact on gambling itself until late 19th-century laws were enacted restricting gambling. The 1920s saw betting on horse-racing re-emerge as restrictions were lifted. The investment in state lotteries of the 1960s and 1970s led to the casinos of the 1990s, which resulted in the multi-billion gaming and casino industry of modern America.

Bertie, Prince of Wales, and Queen Victoria's son and heir apparent, played a great deal of whist for high stakes, losing 138 pounds and seven rubbers, and 101 pounds, as

W.S. Hedges, *A Race Meeting at Jacksonville, Alabama*, 1841, Birmingham Museum of Art, Alabama

recorded in his diary of 1865. Bertie's sister, Alice, was charged by Henry Ponsonby (Queen Victoria's private secretary), and Gladstone, to speak to him about his gambling. Alice, when at Balmoral while Queen Victoria was ill, wrote that the queen was much vexed by Bertie's gambling and thought his behavior would bring the monarchy to an end after her death. Bertie continued to play bridge constantly in the 1909-1910 seasons, according to his diaries. He was considered an indifferent player who had no knowledge of where the cards were, according to Frank Lascelles, who played with him often. Bertie was also alarmingly short tempered with his partners. His lady love, Alice Keppel, teased him by saying she herself "didn't know a king from a knave".

Although Baccarat was illegal in England, the royal family played it every night at Sandringham with a real table and rakes just like those at Monte Carlo. When a table was not available, such as one evening at Tranbycroft, a table was improvised by three whist tables covered by a piece of tapestry. When traveling, Bertie always carried leather counters stamped with £2 or £5l and engraved on the reverse with the Prince of W^aales' feathers.

*North Italian Walnut, Sycamore
and Polychrome Decorated Roulette Table,*
late 18th century

Gambling and Mathematics:
a scientific approach to gaming

Who uses Games shall often prove a loser-
but who falls in love is fettered in fond Cupid's snare.
Isaac Walton, *The Complete Angler*, 1653

● W. R. Richardson, *Twopenny Whist*, 1796

The first analysis of the mathematical possibilities of gambling is thought to have been written by Girolamo Cardano (1501-1576) of Italy, the celebrated mathematician, astrologer, physician, and gambler who discussed dice throwing and its probabilities,. The modern theory of probabilities, though, originated with Blaise Pascal. At the behest of gamblers, Pascal published his findings in *The Laws of Pressure* in 1634.

Abraham de Moivre, an 18th-century French mathematician who lived for many years in England, also studied methods to calculate probabilities and analyzed games of chance such as dice, *il faraone*, *bassetta*, and whist.[35] On an average scale, the dice *can* come up the same three times in succession, negating the laws of probability. A double six is neither rarer nor more frequent than a double four, or any other combination. But for one hundred throws of the dice it does approach the odds of one chance in thirty-six. The odds become apparently sounder for one thousand and even more for one million throws. These rules apply to any gambling game such as roulette.

The outcome of gambling activities like roulette or the act of tossing a coin amount to pure chance, but certain card and board games, notably chess, depend not much on luck, but on strategy: the ability to anticipate and counter one's opponent's moves or the hand dealt.[36] Betting, as we know, makes even a dull game exciting, expressed in the saying *sine periculo friget lusus* or "without danger the game grows cold". The combination of conviviality involving both sexes and the spirit of competition made gambling one of the principal social and intellectual diversions available to our ancestors.

[35] Abraham De Moivre, *The Doctrine of Chances and Method of Calculating the Probabilities of Events in Play* (New York: AMS Chelsea Publishing, 1738).
[36] C.P. Hargrave, *A History of Playing Cards* (New York: Dover Publishing, 2012).

Jan Steen, *The Card Players*, ca. 1660,
oil on canvas, 45.8 x 60.3 cm.
Courtesy Sotheby's

Games as Decorative Objects

*I do not live to play, but I play in order that I may live,
and return with greater zest to the labors of life.*
Plato

Depictions of games and gambling are frequent in the artistic production of Europe. The gaming objects have entire museums devoted to them in Europe, (in France, German, and Belgium, and one in Switzerland at La Tour de Peilz which displays mostly 19th century material).[37]

Game boards in early-modern Europe were sometimes very beautifully made. A 17th-century Bolognese engraver named Giuseppe Maria Mitelli, noted for his satirical engravings, produced images for thirty-three board games. Board games were most popular in the 1600s, especially since dice and card games had become a source of tax revenue and were officially censured, while board games continued to be excluded from the provision of the law. Mitelli's most famous game was the game of *cockaigne* (*cuccagna*) of 1691. It had squares illustrating food specialties from various Italian cities. Throwing number nine resulted in the prize of *cantucci* (the almond *biscotti* of Pisa), number eleven the *gattafura* (a cheese pastry from Genoa), and number fifteen, Paduan bread. The prize for seventeen was nougat from Cremona, although a winner was only allowed to suck on it, not chew. Other prizes were almonds, broccoli from Naples, and cheese from Piacenza. Bologna's *mortadella* was the top prize achieved with triple sixes. Tripe from Milan was the prize for throwing three dice with the number two, and a triple four throw was *mozzarella di bufala* (then originating from Rome). A player won or lost by following instructions written on the square that corresponded to the number the player had thrown with the dice. Some squares dictated forfeits, which could be highly embarrassing, while others

[37] Hotel de Roi de Rome, Rambouillet, France;
Deutsches Soielkarten Museum, Bielefeld, Germany;
Museé National de la Lotterie, Brusselles, Belgium.

allowed the player to impose forfeits on other players.

Destined for Empress Maria Theresa's husband, Francis I, Holy Roman Emperor and Grand Duke of Tuscany in the 18th century, the Medici Grand Ducal manufactory of Florence produced a series of *pietra dura* works based on paintings specially created by Giuseppe Zocchi

● Georges de La Tour, *The Cheat with the Ace of Clubs,* ca. 1630-34, oil on canvas, 97.8 x 152.6 cm. Kimbell Art Museum, Fort Worth, Texas AP 1981.06

● *Noblemen and Women Playing Cards* from Germany, 18th Century, gouache. Private Collection

● Theodor Rombouts, *Card Game,* 1620s, oil on canvas, 143 x 223.5 cm.
The State Hermitage Museum, St. Petersburg

in 1752. These were all reproduced in *pietra dura* and illustrated the leisure pastimes of the aristocratic world and are now conserved at the Museo dell'Opificio delle Pietre Dure in Florence. These stone versions mirrored the paintings and recreated, with hundreds of incredibly accurately hard-cut stones, the nuances of the paintings.

● Johann Georg Platzer, *The Card Players,* ca. 1750, oil on wood, 37.9 x 47.2 cm

Although he only visited Florence once in 1739, Francis I went to the Galleria dei Lavori where they were made. Giuseppe Zocchi was paid for two paintings at a time, beginning in 1751 at the rate of 12 *scudi* each. A large number of artisans were involved at the pietra dura works under the director Louis Siries so that the order could proceed quickly. The *pietra dura* paintings are now in the presidential apartments of the Hofburg Palace in Vienna. A director of the Uffizi Gallery in Florence wrote in 1764: "the Emperor conserves [the game series] jealously after having received them with the pleasure and noble delight of a true sovereign".

THE HISTORY AND DEVELOPMENT OF SPECIFIC GAMES

● Paul Cezanne, *The Card Players*,
1890-95, oil on canvas, 47 x 56,5 cm.
Musée d'Orsay, Paris RF 1969

Cards

*One should always play fairly when one
has the winning cards.*
Oscar Wilde

[1] Also called "money cards", as the earliest cards also functioned as paper currency.
[2] At one time in France, the king of spades was Napoleon and in England, the Duke of Wellington.
[3] Localized card decoration continued well into the nineteenth century. American cards printed during the Civil War depicted suits of Eagles, Shields, Stars, and Flags; face cards included the Goddess of Liberty, a Colonel, and a Major.
[4] "Ace" is a dicing term and an Anglo-Norman word derived from the Latin.

Cards appear to have originated in China between the seventh and tenth centuries.[1] They are first mentioned in an entry in the *Liao Shin* of *T'o-t'o*, a history of the Liao Dynasty (907-1125 A.D.) written in the fourteenth century. According to that source, Emperor Mu played cards on New Year's Eve, 969 A.D. Cards are also thought to be Chinese because of their resemblance to mahjong tiles, despite the very different rules; it is possible that mahjong and dominoes may have developed from early cards. Ancient Chinese cards had four suits and until the fifteenth century in Europe, cards were divided into four suits which corresponded to the four social classes: cups or hearts for clerics, spades or diamonds for merchants, flowers or sticks for peasantry and swords for the military. These designations, considered "French", originated around 1480. There were fifty-six cards in a complete set, ten numbered cards and four figures: the king, queen, cavalier and jack for every "seed" or suit. Local iconography of the four suits had different suit names. Usually the king of spades was a portrait of King David; Charlemagne, the king of hearts; Caesar, the king of diamonds; and Alexander the Great, the king of clubs.[2] Among the Queens were Athena (Pallas or Minerva), Rachel and Judith.[3] The King had the highest value in a card set until the late fifteenth century when the ace became more valuable.[4]

Italy has various regional patterns with Latin or French suits. The Latin version includes *spade* (swords), *coppe* (cups), *bastoni* (batons), and *denari* (coins). The northeastern Italian regions of the Veneto and Friuli have curved swords and straight batons crossed to form a trellis. In the south of Italy, cards have short swords and batons.

Cards follow the French suits in other areas of Italy: *picche* (spades), *fiori* (clubs), *quadri* (diamonds), and *cuori* (hearts). Italian *tarocchi* packs have forty cards with a *Re* (King), *Dama* (Queen), *Fante* (Jack) and are still used in parts of Sicily, Bologna, and Piedmont. The sixty-two-card Bolognese pack was reduced from a seventy-eight-card pack around the early sixteenth century. Popular card games were *scopa* and *scopone*, *terziglio*, *briscola*, *tressetti*, and *madrasso* which was popular in Venice. The Venetians were probably the first to have fifty-six numbered cards rather than the earlier deck of twenty-two.

Venetians, such as Niccolò Polo and his famous son Marco, who traveled to and from China during the thirteenth century, possibly imported cards and dominoes to Europe. In an alternate theory, Moors may have introduced cards to Spain and from there cards spread to the

● *Playing Cards with Money Suits* from China, 1905

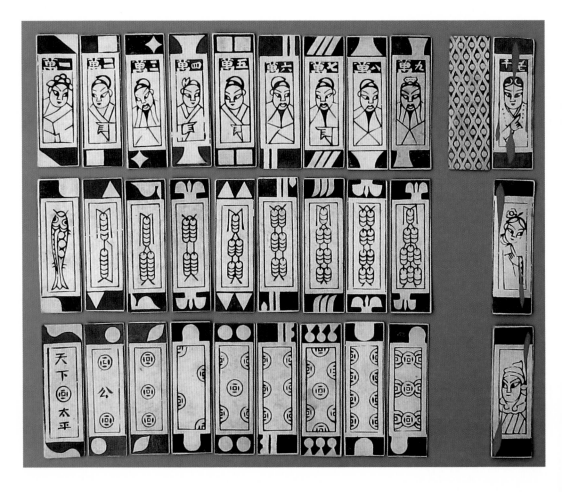

● *Mamlouk Card*, 15th Century.
Topkapi Palace Museum, Istanbul

[5] *Ganjif* is an Indian card game like whist or bridge, with strict rules about which cards can lead. The cards are dealt counter-clockwise to three players (four, if there were twelve or more suits in the packs). Among the materials used for cards were tortoiseshell, ivory, paper, paper mâché, or stiffened fabric, painted by hand. The cards are usually round, from two to twelve centimeters in diameter.

[6] The eight-suited deck may have been a doubling of the pack.

rest of Europe. Ibn Taghri-Birdi's *Annals of Egypt and Syria* of 1417-1418 mentions an episode in which the Sultan al-Malik-al-Mu'ayyad won a great sum of money playing cards, with which he purchased young men. We do know that Spanish cards, or *naipes*, and the earlier term, *naibi*, are derived from the Arabic.

Cards may also have been brought to Egypt in the late fourteenth century by the Mamelukes. The Mameluke deck contained fifty-two cards in four suits like today's deck. The Arabic word *nayb* is actually the name of the second and third court cards in the Mameluke deck. A partial pack was recently found in the Topkapi Museum in Istanbul that matched an already known fragment, forming a complete set. Here the suits were based on the emblems of court life. The word *ganjifa*, meaning "playing card", appeared in the fifteenth century and may be related to the Persian word, *ganj*, or "treasury".[5] Whatever its etymology, the word is said to have been first used for the Mameluke cards and then for the eight-suit packs of Iran and India.[6]

By the end of the Middle Ages, cards had become known throughout Europe. The Canon of the Council of Worcester in 1240 is often quoted as evidence that cards were known in England by the mid-thirteenth century. Many documents mention cards of four suits: in 1370 and 1380 in Germany, Italy, and France. By the late fourteenth century card playing was mentioned in Spanish documents of 1371, Swiss documents in 1377, Florentine documents in 1380, and slightly later in the Netherlands and Germany. A vast iconography of card design was in existence, much of it related to the hunt, including dog collars, hunting horns, knives, buckets, bells, bellows, fish, combs, and numerous other subjects. Many were painted with the heraldic devices of the nobles who commissioned the cards. It was only during the mid-sixteenth century that the designs were standardized.

In 1377, in Basel, Switzerland, a sermon by the Dominican Friar John described a pack of cards. It comprised four seated kings on thrones, each one holding a particular sign in his hand. Under the kings, two *marschalli*, or "marshals", are pictured, the first holding a sign facing upward in the same manner as the kings and the other holding it downward. There were ten other cards of the same size and shape with pips from one to ten for a total of fifty-two cards. This description corresponds to the Egyptian Mameluke pack—which included a first and a second viceroy (*naib*)—and to our modern poker deck.

Some of the names of the card makers are a matter of record, such as Nigel Van Der Noel, to whom the Duchess of Brabant and her husband Duke Wenceslas of Luxembourg paid "two sheep" for cards. Other card-makers to the court of Luxembourg were Colin Greevers and a man known as Geerard. Card games were popular in Flanders and were played for high stakes; indeed, account books state how much money each member of the court lost.

The first documented evidence of cards in what is now Belgium is in the audit office register of the Brussels State Archives and occurs in an entry dated May 14, 1379: at a *fête* in Brussels that year, cards were played, and in May the Receiver General gave the Duke and Duchess four *peters* and two *florins* (valued at a total of eight and one half sheep) to purchase a pack of cards. On June 25, 1379, and later in the year, the receiver paid additional sums to Ange Van Der Noel (possibly a relation of Nigel Van Der Noel) for cards commissioned by the Duchess. Three other packs were delivered in August of 1380 for two half-crowns. In November one of the *servitors* of the Duchess received a *florin* for a similar purchase. Many other entries cite similar sums spent on cards, providing evidence of a craze for cards in 1370s and 80s Flanders.

Such was the case, too, in France. The account books of Charles VI (r. 1380-1422), record payments for the purchase and painting of three decks of cards in various colors and gold (corresponding to nearly one million French francs in mid-twentieth century valuation). An edict was issued prohibiting card games during the workday, and a later edict, issued in Paris on January 22, 1397, forbade working people to play tennis, bowls, dice, nine pins, and cards during the work week. The possessions of the Duc and Duchesse d'Orleans, Louis de Valois and his wife Valentina Visconti included *un jeu de quartes sarrasines* and *un quartes de Lombardie*. In the inventory they were called *quartes* rather than tarots, suggesting that they were probably regular playing cards.

● *Visconti-Sforza Tarot Cards,* ca. 1450-1480, heavy cardboard, 173 x 87 mm. The Morgan Library and Museum, New York MS M.630

Although the earliest European cards were hand painted, by the beginning of the fifteenth century, cards in Germany were produced by block printing. References to these cheaper varieties were made in prohibitions against their use. Easily transportable entertainment, these cards were printed in Europe from carved blocks, a technique formerly used for printing religious texts. Federico di Germania in Bologna seems to have cut blocks for cards as early as 1395. Painted cards had been extremely expensive until the invention of the technique of xylography arrived in the first half of the fifteenth century. Xylography used *pochoirs* or "stencils" to apply colors to cards which gave rise to a new occupation called the *cartier* in France. Lyon and Rouen dominated the market until lithography was invented in 1796.

Cards also appear to have been made in Ulm, Augsburg, and Nuremberg, becoming a regular trade item in fifteenth-century Germany. The terms *kartenmacher* or

● Cards from the *Visconti-Sforza Tarot Cards*, ca. 1450-1480, heavy cardboard, 173 x 87 mm. The Morgan Library and Museum, New York MS M.630

"card-maker" and *formschneider* or "form-cutter" appear on the same page in civic archives and the two professions may have belonged to the same guild.

The manufacture of playing cards also flourished at Tournai, first part of France (from 1187 to 1513), then

⬤ Cards from the *Visconti-Sforza Tarot Cards,* ca. 1450-1480, heavy cardboard, 173 x 87 mm. The Morgan Library and Museum, New York MS M.630

English (until 1519), and then Flemish. Two of the master card makers in Tournai, Michael Noel and Philippe Dubois, formed a guild and registered their personal marks; one claimed a rose, the other a wild boar. The guild stipulated a choice of colors for the cards. Card makers had assistants: those arranging the colors were called *broyeurs* (shredders or grinders), those applying the colors were *bruneteurs,* and those preparing the paper were *carteurs* (carders). Many women worked on card production as well. In Italy, the 1430 income tax return of one such card painter (*pittor di naibi*), Antonio di Giovanni di Ser Francesco of Florence, lists wood blocks used to make playing cards and wood-block images of saints.

The official biographer of Filippo Maria Visconti, third Duke of Milan, wrote in December 1440 that the Duke "enjoyed playing at a game that used painted figures", and expended large sums for cards, paying "1,500 gold pieces to Marziano da Tortona for a pack of cards, with images of gods, emblematic animals and birds". The same master is believed to have painted the famous Visconti di Modrone pack of tarot, or *tarocchi,* cards. Even Albrecht Dürer (1471-1528) at times illustrated tarot cards to supplement his income. Instead of the fifty-two cards of the modern deck, the tarot deck consists of 78 cards and Italian tarot cards typically have sealed or turned over edges. Tarot cards intended to foretell the future are not considered in the same category as playing cards. The earliest tarot cards date from about 1430 and were made for the courts of Mantua and Ferrara.

The Visconti-Sforza tarot decks were commissioned in the fifteenth century and of the original seventy-eight cards, seventy-four have been accounted for. The cards are neither named nor numbered, but those missing are the devil, the tower, the three of swords, and the knight of coins (the devil and the tower are missing possibly because they were deemed unlucky). The Visconti-Sforza deck has a Popess card; she holds a book in her hand and wears the crown of the papacy but her clothes are simple, like those of a nun. The Hermit card was represented as Time holding an hour glass (common in fifteenth-century iconography; later the hour glass would became a lantern). Specific texts were printed with the figures depicted; the top figure was accompanied by *regno* (I reign), the descending figure with *regnavi* (I reigned), the bottom figure with *sum sine regno* (I am without reign), and the ascending figure on the wheel with *regnabo* (I will reign). Fifteenth-century tarot sets still extant from north Italy are much sought after by collectors. A pack attributed to The Master of the Tarot (Visconti) sold for £280,000 at Christie's (Paris) in March, 2005. A Ferrarese tarot trump card from 1470 was sold in Paris at auction for 487,360 francs in 1991.

The Marseille tarot cards, a popular deck that circulated during the sixteenth and seventeenth centuries, featured animal characteristics (such as donkey ears representing foolishness). Later versions depicted the complete animal forms. Nicholas Conver made a woodcut of the set in 1760 that is often used as a model for later sets. Records show that in 1477 a client in Bologna commissioned an artisan named Pietro Tonozzi to make a pack of regular cards and a tarot pack, "hand painted of a particular type with a white back". The contract stipulated the presence of a notary and forbade reproduction of the same card design. Even the colors were outlined in great detail.

Tarot cards from the workshop of Bonificio Bembo, a

Master PW Circular Playing Cards (1499-1515)

painter from Cremona, were commissioned by the court of the Milanese dukes. Bembo's cards were covered with burnished gold then painted with tempera, a technique that provided a delicate luminosity and fine finish. A nearly complete set is at the Pinacoteca di Brera in Milan and is named after its last owner, Giovanni Brambilla. The Colleoni-Baglioni deck, one of the most famous tarot collections, is now divided between the Pierpont Morgan Library & Museum in New York and the Accademia Carrara in Bergamo, Italy.[7]

It was only in 1781 that tarot cards acquired mystical significance. A former Protestant pastor and freemason, Antoine Court de Gébelin, published *Le monde primitif analysé et comparé avec le monde moderne*, in which he claimed that tarot was a secret and philosophical doctrine containing the mysteries of ancient Egyptian priesthoods. French occultist Jean-Baptiste Alliette, writing under the pseudonym "Esteilla", designed tarot cards specifically used to foretell the future. Tarot cards are still used for divination by fortune-tellers in the Western world, especially in central Europe.

In Medieval and Renaissance Europe, card-playing led to gambling which attracted the attention and disapproval of ecclesiastical and civic authorities. On May 23, 1376 a type of card game called *naibbe* was forbidden in Florence by a decree outlawing gambling. Passionate players tolerated the discomfort of bad weather, the cold or the heat, as games were played everywhere. In fourteenth century Florence, a grocer was accused of holding illegal card games in his shop; the customers placed their bets while sitting on large drums of Parmesan and other cheeses. Roving patrols of police reported these events.

Saint Bernardino preached a sermon, in the cathedral

[7] Later examples of tarot packs from Lombardy reveal similarities to the earlier 'Saracen' cards, strengthening the hypothesis of the Islamic origins of playing cards.

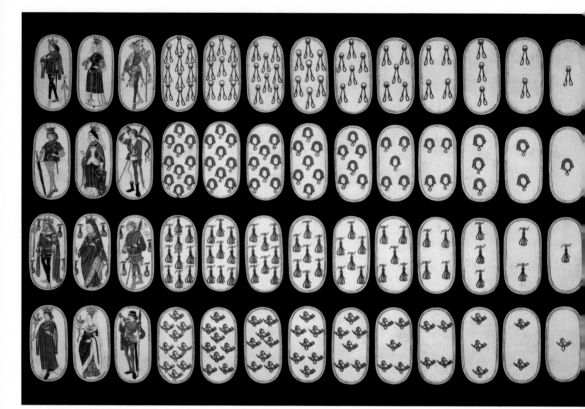

of San Petronio, Bologna, against gaming in general and playing cards in particular (he specifically described a pack of fifty-six cards, including queens). He tried to persuade players to burn their cards and when some of his followers threw their cards into the fire, a card maker present exclaimed, "I have not learned, Father, any other business than that of painting cards, and if you deprive me of that, you deprive me of life, and my destitute family of the means to earn a subsistence!" Saint Bernardino promptly replied, "If you do not know what to paint, paint this figure and you will never have cause to repent having done so", and he showed the card maker an image of a radiant sun, centered by the holy monogram "IHS".

Denunciations of card playing continued throughout the Renaissance. Card shops in particular were targeted. Pietro Aretino, in his satirical work *I Ragionamenti*, published in 1534-1536, describes the instructive pornographic frescoes on the walls of a convent-brothel which illustrated Saint Nafissa who used a card shop as her place to sleep

Playing Cards from Burgundy, ca. 1470-80, The Cloisters, Metropolitan Museum of Art, New York

with a variety of men: police, spies, priests, and footmen.

In Girolamo Savonarola's Bonfire of the Vanities of 1497 in Florence, a considerable part of the bonfires consisted of cards and gaming tables. In a similar occurrence, after a 1452 sermon in Nuremburg, a large quantity of games, forty thousand dice, and a greater number of cards were burned in the marketplace.

Some playing cards were circular, such as those made by the Master P.W. in Cologne around 1470. They comprised seventy-two cards of four suits; kings and queens, roses, carnations, rabbits or hares, parrots, and cherubim were pictured at the top of the cards. The kings and queens were mounted on horseback and the kings were differentiated by the placement of their suit signs either on the upper or lower part of the card. The upper card showed a running figure, and the lower, a standing one.

English card decks, with which we are most familiar, had, and still have, the kings, queens, and knights dressed in the fashion of the time of Henry VII. In England, cards were included among a motley collection of wares subject to importation fees: fire tongs, dripping pans, dice, tennis balls, pins, pattins, pack needles, painted wares, daggers, wood knives, bodkins, tailor's sheers, razors, and *cartes à jouer*. These items were controlled and duties levied to safeguard local trades. Card playing was prohibited by statute on March 4, 1463 from Michaelmas, the 11th of September, until September 29th, 1464, but, in time, cards became a source of government revenue in England—as it had been in France for Charles VII—when James I of England (r. 1603-1625) taxed both imported and local production of cards. In England, after 1765, the tax levied was printed on the ace of spades, leading producers and players to invent methods to avoid paying the tax. Their ploys included forging the ace of spades and making secondhand sales of the cards.

In Tuscany, each card had to be stamped with a tax and an identification of origin and players caught with unstamped cards could be punished. Tuscany's borders were monitored for the importation of illicit cards. Cards were sometimes forged and card sharks sometimes added tiny pinpricks or marked the cards in other ways to facilitate cheating.

At the Medici Art Academy in the Palazzo Madama, Rome, an employee who had witnessed students' illicit card games was slapped and punched repeatedly by the young men. When Cosimo III de' Medici was informed, he was shocked. The young Florentine artists begged the compassion of the serene patron and became "models of respect, diligence, and good behavior, all being filled with terror that they [could] be dismissed for the slightest failing".[8]

In *Capitolo del gioco della primiera col' comento de Messer Pietro-Paolo de San Chirico*, a book attributed to Francesco Berni, a card game called *primiera* was praised as the most interesting and noble of them all.[9] Other card games were called *ronfa, la cricca, i trionfi, il flusso, il trentuno,* and *la bassetta* (which the author considered too violent). The opinionated Berni called chess and backgammon *gioco de gottosi,* "games for those with gout"!

A popular game in Venice, *Trieze* or "thirteen", was mentioned by William Beckford (1760-1844): "*Trieze* is the [Venetians'] favorite game; *uno, due, tre, cinque, fante, cavallo, re,* are eternally repeated; the apartments echoed no other sound. I wonder a lively people can endure such monotony—and so eager in the pursuit of amusement as hardly to allow themselves any sleep".[10]

In 1616, a special tax was levied on playing cards in Venice, instigated by woodcutters and playing-card makers who asked for the city council's protection against imported cards which they claimed were ruining their trade. Their request was granted and the import of every kind of print (including those for textiles) was forbidden; the penalty was a seizure of the articles and a fine. A two *soldi* tax per card pack was levied without "any prejudice on the 7% entry duty and exit fee on the thick paper that served to fabricate cards". In 1652 this duty was raised dramatically to sixteen *soldi,* an order that seems to have been aimed at German card makers.[11]

In England, Frank Willoughby's seventeenth-century book of games described rules for *tick tack*, backgammon, and instructions for making playing cards: "three or four pieces of white paper, pasted together smoothly, so they may slip easily from one another. If they grow dark, they must be dried and rubbed, one by one, to make them

8   Letter. 12 December 1685. ASF Medici Princes 3951. 5 January 1686 Mancini to Bassetti. ASF Medici Princes 3952.
9   *Qual altro ha più grandezza, più galanteria, più generosità e più libertà di questo* (Rome, 1526).
10   William Beckford, *Italy with Sketches of Spain and Portugal* (Cambridge, Mass.: Harvard University Press, 1834).
11   Joseph Ottley, *An Enquiry into the Origin and Early History of Engraving Upon Copper and Wood* (1816), p. 48.

THE HISTORY AND DEVELOPMENT OF SPECIFIC GAMES

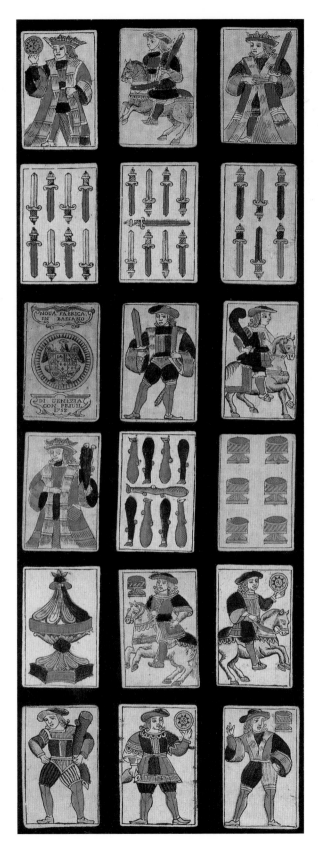

Remondini di Bassano, *Playing Cards*, 1775. Museo della Stampa Remondini, Bassano del Grappa

slip again". In 1660, after a lengthy exile abroad, Charles II brought with his reign a bent for gambling and merriment. After years of civil war and a puritan theocracy, it was a welcome change for the English people. The whist authority Edmond Hoyle (1672-1769) codified the rules for card playing which are still referred to as "according to Hoyle". Along with the card games, unfortunately, came professional card sharks and cheats.

During the 1720s, the Countess of Bristol, who had a very generous salary as a Lady of the Bed Chamber for the Princess of Wales, was addicted to gambling. According to Lady Montague, "[the Countess of Bristol] was transformed when she managed to get up from the card table, being resolved to make up for time misspent, she had two lovers at a time".[12] It was said that King George II's favorite games were commerce and backgammon: "He plays between nine and eleven at night with his daughter, Amelia, and his mistress Amelie. The queen plays quadrille". King George II's mistress Delaraine, also played cards nightly with the German courtier August Schutz: "winning money at cards was the highest hope of pleasure".[13]

Despite his many mistresses, King George II was extremely devoted to his wife, Queen Caroline. After her death, he was unable to speak of his wife without weeping,

[12] Lucy Worsley, *Courtier: The Secret History of Kensington Palace* (London: Faber & Faber, 2010), p. 49.
[13] Letter by Lady Montague.

and "on his daughters' orders, the queen card was removed from George II's pack of cards. The sight of the queen card put him into so great a disorder".[14]

One's skill at playing cards and reputation for gambling were widely known at the English court. Lord Chesterfield wrote of the satirical writer and physician Dr. John Arbuthnot that: "[t]he doctor played two games against a dog and was most shamefully beaten", and mutual friends joked that Arbuthnot, "the inept gambler, and John Gay [an impecunious poet and hanger-on at court], both had unfortunate vices. Doctor goes to cards, Gay to court. One loses money, one loses time".[15]

Peter Wentworth, who managed the public lottery, described the court routine at Kensington Palace under George II as: "dinner at three and start from the table, a little after five for a walk. At six, everyone returned and sat down to cards in the drawing room".[16] Wentworth died suddenly, as reported on January 12, 1739 in the *London Evening Post,* half-way through a hand of *quadrille.*

For the general populace, King George II recommended the suppression of night houses, gin shops, tipling houses, gaming tables and Sir John Conson's campaign against "vices, immorality and profanities" instructed all bawdy houses, disorderly houses, unlicensed ale houses and gaming houses to be closed.

In Italy, a popular Venetian card game was *Meneghella* or "Joker'. It was described by the playwright Carlo Goldoni (1707-1793) in the introduction to his comedy *Una delle Ultime Sere di Carnevale* (One of the Last Evenings of Carnival). It was played with a fifty-two card Italian deck, including the *meneghella,* by a maximum of sixteen people divided into pairs. Each player could see their partner's cards. The bets were placed provisionally on a central plate and whoever had the highest value card became the dealer. Each player received cards, the dealer held six for himself and chose the three highest from these. A card was then pulled from those left out of the distribution. The holder of the *meneghella,* which had the highest value, received all the money. If the card was not played, the remainder of the deck was passed to the next player, who would put out his or her highest card after consulting a partner. The other players were then obliged

[14] Lord Ed Hailes, *The Opinions of Sarah, Duchess Dowager of Marlborough* (1788).
[15] Lucy Worsley, *Courtier: The Secret History of Kensington Palace* (London: Faber & Faber, 2010), p. 101.
[16] In a 1729 letter to his brother.

to put out a card of equal value. Whoever won took one third of the bets in the middle of the table, followed by the second winner. The third winner would start the wagers again. The others could trump the card played; sometimes low cards were played to"scare" adversaries. When the third hand was played, the deck was passed to the next player.

Quadrille was perfected in eighteenth-century France— it was a four-handed version of the Spanish game *ombre*— and became a fashionable game around 1726. It remained so for over a hundred years in Europe and England until whist (a forerunner of bridge) became popular. Quadrille was a complex game, had an upside-down ranking system in two suits, non-standard bids and scoring of extreme complexity. The game consisted in any number of deals divisible by four. Before each deal the player placed a chip into the pot or the dealer staked four. The game passed to the right and players received ten cards dealt in two groups of threes and one of fours. Counting chips—usually finely made and similar to coins with a center hole— were necessary accessories for games such as quadrille. Quadrille card boxes contained four smaller boxes, each marked with a suit which held lacquered wood or ivory *fiche* (a narrow, flat stick) also marked either clubs, hearts, spades, or diamonds. These could be exquisitely made, especially in mid-eighteenth century Venice. Though rare, some counting chips have survived.

A gifted engraver to Louis XV worked on counter boxes for the game of quadrille. They were engraved in ivory with dolphins on the lids (the dolphin referred to the *dauphin*, the son of the King). Examples of these variously colored boxes are at the Rijksmuseum in Amsterdam (a signed box along with its place of origin, Rouen), the Fitzwilliam Museum in Cambridge (UK) and the Deutsches Museum of Bielefeld.

The *Confraternita dell'arte Vaginer* (box-makers guild) had a *scuola*, or headquarters, designed by Jacopo Sansovino (1486-1570), the renowned architect of the Mint, the Campanile, and the Library of San Marco. At the annual celebration of the Ascension in August, called *la Sensa*, the box-makers, or *vagineri*, displayed their wares in wooden structures especially designed for the event under the sign

● *French Counting Boxes,* ca. 1720, gilded and painted wood, ivory fiche. Private Collection

of the *confraternita.* The boxes were made of simple materials but very well-constructed. They were beautifully decorated with the Venetians' distinct light touch by the *dipintori,* or "lacquer painters", an art which reached its height in the mid-eighteenth century. Box decorations were floral or in the *chinoiserie* style, or of gallant and pastoral scenes. In 1754 there were twenty-five lacquer masters; by 1779 there were forty-nine. In addition, there were about thirty-five workshops with another fifty lacquer workers, all fueled by the fashion for cards and other games. Another style of box decoration was *arte povera* (also called *lacca contraffatta* and decalcomania), with its skillfully and minutely cut-out engravings, evidence of incredibly skillful work. The engravings were arranged on the object, glued, and then painted and lacquered. Aristocrats took to carrying gold scissors on a chain, so that they might cut out engravings for application on luxurious objects when paying visits.

In Italy much artistry and expense went into the making of lavish card tables. Some of these are astonishing examples of the art of marquetry and inlay featuring "paintings" made of precious woods. Northern Italian artisans, such as Gaetano Renoldi and Giovanni Maffezzoli, created superb examples with classical scenery and amorous poetry as part of the design, as illustrated here.

Card playing—and its attendant activity, gambling—was all the rage in Paris where cards of every type were available. The tutor to the young Louis XIV (r. 1643-1715) used cards to teach his pupil the names of the kings and queens of France and to help him learn heraldry, geography, and Greek mythology. A game conceived by Desmarets de Saint-Sorlin and engraved by Stefano della Bella in 1664 depicted the kings of France.

Geographic maps of reduced scale were made by Pierre du Val and sold as a set of cards called *Geographe du Roy* in 1669. The *Ancien Régime* saw a variety of portraits of the dauphin depicted on the cards from Auvergne, Burgundy, Lyons, and Paris. Other cards with political agendas were made as well, from the *cartes royales* of historical kings and queens made in 1815 by A.G. Houligant, to the Game of Flags of 1816, and cards produced in 1830 on the occasion of the barricades.[17]

During the reign of Louis XIV, Parisian society was consumed with card games. In Madame Deshoulières' book on gaming she wrote, "one begins by being a dupe, one ends by being a rascal".[18] In Paris, one of the first collectors of paintings by Teniers, Brouwer, and Breughel wrote in his memoirs (in the second half of the seventeenth century) about being caught cheating at cards, and his subsequent exile. He took religious orders at Saint Benoit-Sur-Loire, where he continued gambling and was driven out to finish his days at the lunatic asylum of Sainte-Lazare.

Henri de Campion, a Norman gentleman who wrote his memoirs in the early seventeenth century, excelled at gambling once he abandoned dice for backgammon and card games. Although he considered games of chance nobler, they were also riskier, and his "honest skill", through both fortune and misfortune, ultimately reaped

17   In 1830, the iconographer M. Hebin, taking apart a book binding, found a fifteenth-century playing card. Cards as old as this are now very rare.
18   *On commence par être dupe, on finit par être fripon.* Deshoulières, *Réflexions sur le jeu* (1688).

○ *Venetian Game Box,* with four smaller boxes and counting chips, ca. 1725-35. Private Collection

○ *French mid sixteenth century cards* from Rouen

its reward.[19] De Campion confessed in his memoirs that he loved both gambling and winning and avowed that although he was not of a quarrelsome nature, he was always tempted to join in his friends' gaming quarrels.

The model for the noble gentleman *d'épée* (sword) was described by the Chevalier, Comte de Gramont (1621-1707) as the following: "His gaiety, his disdain for economy, his passion for gaming, his sumptuous expenses, his appetite for gallant intrigues, his talents, loving charms, his spirit, his valor, and a touch of cynicism were the traits most admired in the high nobility". A taste for gambling was a virtue among the fashionable nobility.

François Roget de Gaignières, a seventeenth century enlightened thinker and tutor to the royal children, had a

● Hubert-François Bourguignon (Gravelot), *A Game of Quadrille*, ca. 1740, oil on canvas, 63.5 x 76.2 cm. Yale Center for British Art, New Haven B2011.34

[19] Henri de Campion, *Memoires* (1807).

THE HISTORY AND DEVELOPMENT OF SPECIFIC GAMES

collection of playing cards, according to Dr. Lister, a zoologist and antiquarian who visited him in 1698, "some of which were three hundred years old!".[20] Today, however, no complete card packs made before the seventeenth century are extant.

King Louis XIV at first thought that gambling was a good distraction for the courtiers who languished at Versailles, and would perhaps make them even more dependent on him. The king often had to pay the debts of family members, his brother, for example, never contested any decision he made. By 1679, however, Louis XIV had prohibited gambling (although it still went on in the nobles' private quarters).

A letter by Madame de Sèvigné (1626-1696) described the separation of Madame de La Sablière and her reluctant lover La Fare, a crisis caused by the popular card game *bassette*:

> It was *bassette*, would you believe it? It was in the name of *bassette* that faithlessness was declared; he abandoned religious adoration for the sake of the prostitute, *bassette*. The moment had come for this passion to cease, even to be transferred to another object; can one believe that *bassette* could be anyone's path to salvation? She looked first at this distraction, this desertion; she examined all the bad excuses, the insincere reasoning, the pretexts, the embarrassed self-justification, the uncomfortable conversations, the impatience to leave her company, the journeys to Saint-Germain where he gambled, the weariness, the no longer knowing what to say; finally, when she had carefully observed the eclipse that was taking place... La Fare plays *bassette*. *Et le combat finit faute de combattants.*[21]

Pharaon (also *faraone*, or *faraon*) in Italian, was considered a new game in early eighteenth-century France, but it was little more than the game of *bassette* (which had been forbidden thirty years earlier) revived with another name! *Pharaon* was one of the most popular games and played constantly in *salons*. In the game of *pharaon*, two cards were dealt and the banker took in all the bets placed on the cards corresponding to those at their left. The banker then paid those which corresponded to the bets placed to

[20] "The oldest card was three times bigger than those now used ... extremely well lined and illuminated with gilt borders, and the pasteboard thick and firm, but there was not a complete set of them". Dr. Martin Lister, *A Journey to Paris in 1680.*
[21] "and the battle ends for to lack of combatants", Letter from Mme de Sévigné to Mme de Grignan, July 14, 1680.

● *Playing Cards with a Revolutionary Theme*, 18th Century. Musée Carnavalet, Paris 01-016243

his right. The sums placed on different cards of the first pair were moved to those remaining in the game and then the game proceeded to other pairs and bets.[22] During his visit to Turin, Prèsident de Brosses described a variation of *pharaon*:

> Houses and gatherings were both brilliant and numerous: they play *pharaon* in a very singular manner. The banker is a high-level hawker. He puts the bank into a box garnished with trinkets (scraps of gold jewelry, the worst quality he can find) each of which has a numbered price, which never is less than double its real value. The winning cards

22 The difference between *bassette* and *faraon* was that in *bassettes* the banker decided on the placement and not the players.

● Roger Vandercruz Lacroix,
Louis XVI Transitional Table.
Private Collection

● *Right*, Italian trômpe l'œil,
18 Century, tempera. Private
Collection

are paid with a choice of these jewels. When they lose, however, they pay with money. I leave you to decide if the mechanism was invented to reestablish egalitarianism in this so disadvantaged game. There is also, in the way the game is played, a difference from ours. We pay half the bet on the doublet. Here the banker draws all. In revenge, when our card loses *sonica* you only pay one third of the bet. One must observe these sorts of gatherings are everywhere.[23]

Another game commonly played was *jeu de la mauch*, played with thirty-two cards by three to four people or with fifty-two cards for five to six players. The winning player had to have twenty round and sixteen rectangular chips (the long chips were valued as the equivalent of five of the round chips).

Toward the end of Louis XIV's reign, Versailles offered endless gambling for the courtiers during social evenings in the king's apartment, three times a week for about

23   Prèsident de Brosses, *Voyage en Italie* 1739 *Vol. 1-2.* Lettre LVIII.

● *Plate with Playing Card Decoration*, 1780, earthenware and polychrome. Sèvres, Cité de la céramique

three hours called *appartent*. Music was played, then games; card games including *la cavagnole*, as well as billiards, while lavish refreshment was available in a separate salon. Great gamblers such as the Dowager Queen of France (Anne of Austria) and Cardinal Mazarin were present. Indeed, social advancement could be achieved through gambling skills. The Marquis de Dangeau, for example, was admired for his gambling prowess: "Nothing distracts him. He neglects nothing, he profits by everything".[24] Monsieur de Seissac, an inveterate cheater, had marked cards substituted for the regular deck by his valets. When found out, he was stripped of his titles and expelled from the court and from Paris; he was, however, five hundred thousand *écus* the richer, a sum which must have helped in his exile.

Brelan (also *breland*) was a famous French vying card game, featuring rapidly raised bets, similar to *bouillotte*. Brelan was mentioned in an edict in Lille of 1458 and it continued to be popular from the 1600's through the nineteenth century. Crebillon's 1763 novel, *Le Hasard du coin du feu* featured brelan as a central theme. The rules

[24] The Marquis was also a renowned jester; he resembled Louis XIV and was able to convincingly impersonate him. Antonia Fraser, *Love and Louis XIV: The Women in the Life of the Sun King* (New York: Random House, 2006), p. 237.

Du Paquier Porcelain Manufactury Gaming Set, 1735-40, hard-paste porcelain, polychrome enamels, gild mounts, diamonds, 16.8 x 14.8 cm. Art Institute of Chicago, Chicago 1993.349

for the game varied, but generally a pack of thirty-two cards was used and played by three, four or five players, each receiving three cards. A fourth card was turned from the stack; four of a kind with the aid of the turn-up card determined the best hand. Unlike bouillotte, which lasts as long as the players haven't lost their stakes, *brelan cave* is limited to a certain number of rounds. Brelan is related to the French game of *gilet* (*gillet, gile* or *trionfetti*), considered the origins of poker.

Tray Decorated with Playing Cards, 18th Century. The British Museum, London

Bouillotte came into its own at the time of the Revolution in France.[25] The French bouillotte table was invented solely for the purpose of playing this game and is still a much-desired classic of French furniture. The table is round with a pierced brass gallery, marble top, sometimes a wooden pedestal base—usually mahogany—or more commonly, four fluted legs. It has a drawer on either side and two pull-out slides; occasionally it has a removable top that fits over the marble with baize—a coarse, woolen cloth like that used on billiard tables—on the underside. The bouillotte lamp was also popularized at this time. It had a gilded brass pedestal base, often pierced, and *tôle*, or metal, shade, painted dark green. The lamp had one, two, or three candle holders and a shade which could be lowered as the candles burned down. The lamps are also still much sought after. Cards have remained an important device in decorations, from hard stone table tops, *scagliola*, designs for wood inlay, and for ceramic decoration in many European countries.

[25] The open-card stud variation in poker was influenced by bouillotte. Except when five people played, a picquet pack of twenty cards was used with the removal of the sevens, tens and jacks. In the case of three players, the queens were also removed. The player with an ace chose where to sit first. In America, where the game was popular after 1830, the first dealer held the king card.

🔵 *Scagliola Table Decorated with Playing Cards* from Carpi, mid-18th Century, top 120 x 57 cm. Private Collection

The clergy in France and England, while they had previously considered card playing harmless and even played themselves, later came to condemn it. In America, Puritans considered the mere *possession* of playing cards a vice, and punished those they caught playing the game of whist. Benjamin Franklin wrote in *Poor Richard's Almanac* (1736) that, "a man gets no thanks for what he loseth at play". More disapproving was Thomas Jefferson, who told his wife, Martha, in a letter that, "gaming corrupts our dispositions and teaches us a habit of hostility against all mankind". On the other hand Lord Byron (1788-1824), took a more philosophic (and poetic) view: "in play there are two pleasures for your choosing, the one is winning and the other losing".

Important collections of playing cards were being formed in the seventeenth century. The Parisian Roger de Gaignières had a collection of celebrated tarot cards dating from the end of the fifteenth century which attracted foreigner visitors. At his death, his collection was bequeathed to the *Bibliothèque du Roi*, afterwards to the *Bibliothèque Nationale de France*, and included rare seventeenth-century card decks.[26]

In Russia, whist was the standard after-dinner pastime at the court of Catherine the Great. The Empress's favorite game, however, was ombre, the fashionable three-hand game of Spanish origin whose addictive power was satirized by the poet Vasily Markov. Catherine wrote to Moscow's Governor General that, "the noble who squandered his money gambling will be obliged to sell his village, other nobles, lacking sufficient recourses will be in no position to buy, and, in that case, the only remaining purchaser will be manufacturers, so you are to make sure that no games of chance are played, and confirm to the police that the published edicts about this are to be precisely enforced".[27] However, on Catherine's trip south where the company included many foreigners, it "descended into hedonistic excess"; a Russian was said to have won 28,000 rubles at cards once the party had left St. Petersburg.[28] On the other hand, import duties on foreign playing cards and a tax on Russian-made packs led the College of Commerce to promise combined annual revenue of 12,000 rubles in 1765.

[26] The Musèe Français de la Carte à jouer at d'Issy-les-Moulineaux near Paris is dedicated to the playing card and its history.
[27] Simon Dixon, *Catherine the Great* (New York: Ecco, 2009).
[28] *Ibid.*

Giuseppe Verdi and the librettist Francesco Maria Piave included a card game in the 1853 opera *La Traviata*. In one scene, Violetta's former lover challenges her new love Alfredo to a card game and proceeds to lose a small fortune to him, winnings which Alfredo will later throw at Violetta's feet. An avid card player, Igor Stravinskij (1882-1971) created a ballet called *Jeux des cartes* in 1937, with choreography by George Balanchine (1904-1983) in which the action takes place in three "deals". Act IV of Jules Massenet's opera *Manon* (1884) includes a gambling scene where Manon suggests to her former lover that he recoup his lost fortune by gambling. He wins at cards but is accused of cheating. The police arrest him, and Manon as his accomplice. After begging forgiveness for the shame she has brought him, she dies in his arms. A fitting punishment for the sin of gambling, in nineteenth-century French opera!

Cards are still one of the main leisure activities for peo-

● Johann Rudolf Feyerabend, *Still Life with Fruit, Kitchenware and Dominos*, 18th Century, oil on canvas. Private Collection

ple of all ages and in every social sphere. An International Playing Card Society exists with thousands of members. Bridge has developed into a source of study and professional competition. In some schools, students accustomed to solitary activities on computers and smart phones are being taught to play bridge. While chess is still the game of choice amongst educators, bridge is seen as offering similar mental benefits. Teachers say that bridge improves the students' social skills, forcing them to collaborate with a partner, which appeals to many children. Bridge is considered a tool to teach math in a new way, by developing critical thinking, inferential reasoning, and problem-solving skills. Having seventh and eighth grade pupils concentrating for three hours is a phenomenon of bridge, teachers say. In 2009 a nine-year-old named Richard Jeng became the youngest life master in the history of the American Contract Bridge League where the average age of the 165,000 members is 67.

Johann Rudolf Feyerabend, *Still Life with Fruit, Kitchenware and Playing Cards*, 18th Century, oil on canvas. Private Collection

Venetian Game Box, with four smaller
boxes and counting chips, ca. 1725-35.
Private Collection

Lotteries and Gambling

Keep flax from fire, youth from gaming.
Benjamin Franklin, *Poor Richard's Almanack,* 1736

In sixteenth-century Italy lotteries were used as a means to raise money for armies. The Milanese Ambrosian Republic offered lottery prizes of up to 200 *ducats* drawn from the *borsis ventura,* or "bag of fortune", in 1448. Buyers purchased tickets on which they wrote their names and won a prize if their ticket was drawn. By the mid-sixteenth century, Rome, Genoa and Venice also had several lotteries. Roman legislation made it obligatory to show the prize before the purchase of the ticket. Edicts forbade all *lotteria ò ventura,* or "lottery of fortune" without a license.

The first lotteries in Venice appeared around the Rialto Bridge. Lotteries had been condemned by the *Consiglio del Dieci* (Council of Ten), the highest authority of the Venetian government, which had also issued a decree forbidding the new game of lotto. The authorities initially thought to suppress lotteries due to the great losses suffered by some players. The prohibition was generally ignored and the Rialto lotteries continued despite the threat to confiscate the prizes. The government, however, soon reversed itself and began sponsoring lotteries when the city needed funds, a practice that continued throughout the eighteenth century. Lotteries were sometimes sponsored by private citizens (without permission) until the state forbade them.

In 1522, the Venetian government offered jewels and silk from Cyprus by lottery, and, in 1523 offered wood groves in Lignago on the *terraferma,* the mainland. By the late 1520s taxes on wine, sugar and products from butchers and fishmongers were sold by lottery ticket. By the end of the sixteenth century, new shops in the Rialto in

Venice were sold using lottery tickets. Preventing unauthorized lotteries proved difficult, despite potential fines of up to 200 *ducats* or six months in prison.

At one time the inventory of the Venetian Dolfin family was put to a lottery (probably after a bankruptcy claim in 1570) by the *Provedidori del Comune*. There were 8,000 lots worth an estimated 100,000 *ducats* including jewels, silver, gold, furnishings such as carved and gilded chairs with red velvet cushions, tapestries, silk, wool cloth, a house in Udine worth 2,400 *ducats*, and silver basins, ewers and cups bearing the Dolfin coat of arms.

At the Rialto, Marin Sanudo noticed a new type of gaming in which small amounts of money and valuables were placed in trust to chance. He described the activity in his diaries:

> It started off as a low-level thing by the second-hand dealer, Girolomo Bambara, and has now grown. First, anyone who wanted gave twenty *soldi*, then 3 *lire* and then a *ducat*. They put up prizes, carpets, wall hangings, and other things. Now, they are putting up silver worth 200 *ducats*, and others have put up gold, charging a *ducat* per name. And it is done in this way: whoever wants to participate writes on a piece of paper and hands over the money. Everyone gathers in a certain shop chosen for this purpose, where there are two bags with as many slips that say patience (*patientia*). When everyone is gathered, they call in a small boy and having mixed the slips well in the sacks, the youth then takes out a name from the first sack and then goes to the second. If he pulls out a slip with a "prize", the person wins. If he pulls out the slip that says *patientia* he gains nothing and has lost. Thus, everyday in Rialto there is someone doing this.

In 1550 the artist Lorenzo Lotto organized a lottery in Ancona (there was less regulation in smaller towns) offering sixteen paintings and thirty intarsia designs as prizes. Lotto sold a remarkable 884 tickets for seven paintings and raised 44 *scudi* and four *bolognini*, making a profit of 40 *scudi*. The element of chance involved made this akin to gambling and the magistrates soon recognized that the lotteries were new forms of games of chance. Gambling, as

● Pietro Longhi, *Il Ridotto*, ca. 1750s, oil on canvas, 84 x 115 cm. Fondazione Scientifica Querini Stampalia, Venice

opposed to gaming, involved no skill and was widely condemned.

Biribissi, however, was the most ruinous pastime in many places. The game of *biribi* (also called *biribissi*, *biribiss*, and *biribisso*) required a decorated board for play, but was a game of chance like a lottery and was an early version of roulette. It was often played in noble circles in Italy beginning in the sixteenth century and in France from the seventeenth century. The *biribissi board* was divided into several sections of various numbers, usually thirty-six numbered sections, each with a figure or device to distinguish them. Thirty-six or more numbers were written on paper, tightly rolled and placed in small, wooden, olive-shaped forms pierced with a central hole and enclosed in a drawstring bag. The banker held the covered bag to impede the view of these "olives". A number was extracted—the papers could be pushed out by a turned ivory stick—and the number written on it was announced. The player who had placed his or her bet on the slot corresponding to the

number won. The banker had only to execute the bet and give the winner thirty-two, thirty-six, or sixty-four times their wager and gather the losing bets.

In his memoirs, Giacomo Casanova (1725-1798) recalled playing *biribiss* in a private house in Genoa (where, as in Venice, the game was prohibited). That evening, he recounted, he always bet on the harlequin figure, normally corresponding to the number eight, and wrote that it came up three times consecutively on his three turns. He claimed it was pure luck, which is possible.[1]

In *biribissi*, the bank was overseen by three people: one distributed the money, another held the bag with the olives, and a third took in money for bets placed. The players extracted the olives themselves with the right hand, taking three turns before passing on to the next player. The number of players could be unlimited.[2] The ancestor of bingo and lotto, this variant of *cavagnole* and a

⦿ Pietro Longhi, *Card Players*, 1760, oil on canvas. Galleria d'Arte Moderna, Milan

[1]   Giacomo Casanova, *Mémoires, Volume I-II* (1789).
[2]   Paintings of biribissi scenes attributed to the Master of the Biribiss (previously attributed to Marco Marcuolo) show the playing of the game in mostly outdoor settings.

game called *trou-madame* was popular in France until it was prohibited in 1837.

In France during the *Régence* (1715-1723) and the reign of Louis XV (r. 1715-1774), aristocrats prized the ownership of fine game accessories for games such as biribissi, elaborately embroidered velvet drawstring purses, tinted ivory chips, or flat *fiche,* and little ivory sticks to poke into the black olive forms to extract the paper within. Although the chips were smaller, they are similar to the chips used in casinos today.

In Italy, Louis XV's daughter, the Duchess of Modena, liked to play *le biribi* all night, have supper at six o'clock in the morning, and to go to bed two hours later. Consequently, she got up at five in the afternoon, attended to her affairs and returned to the gaming tables at seven in the evening. The Marchese Bevilacqua remarked that he did not find this routine as pleasant as she, and complained of the disorder this lifestyle brought to the Modenese court: "The duchess gave all her energies to *biribi* in her lodge. The *fermier* [Minister of Agriculture] of the state . . . held the bank of the *biribi* and placed the bets,

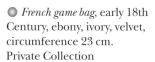 *French game bag,* early 18th Century, ebony, ivory, velvet, circumference 23 cm. Private Collection

which is to say that he passed the night being given the quittances".[3]

A *Ridotto* (from *redorsi* or 'to meet'), a gambling place for nobles existed near Piazza San Marco as early as 1282. From the early thirteenth century, gambling locations were regulated until they were finally prohibited by the magistrate of the *esecutori* (executors). In 1296, a law was passed in Venice against playing where wine was sold; the fine was one hundred *soldi*, one third of which would be given to the accuser. Priests and clergymen who gambled, even excessively, were immune to fines and punishments related to gaming. In the thirteenth and fourteenth centuries, gaming while sitting on the street and on bridges throughout the city was not unusual. A traveler named Coryat, visiting Venice in 1608, noted a sign in Piazza San Marco allowing a certain Nicola Baretterius a place to play or gamble legally between two columns in the piazza.[4]

The Palazzo Dandolo, near the piazza San Marco, housed the *Ridotto Pubblico di San Moisè*, which opened in 1638 as a public gaming house and was administered by the state as part of their efforts to control gambling and to profit from the activity. The Ridotto was open to all citizens and foreigners during the Carnival period. The *croupiers*, or bankers, were exclusively patrician and were allowed to lend money to players but were not permitted to wear masks in the Ridotto (for fear of espionage).[5] Private companies and usurers also provided sums to the gamblers. Gamblers at the Ridotto, however, had to be masked. To reserve a table or consume refreshments in the game rooms was prohibited.[6] In eighteenth-century Venice, patricians were allowed to "make bank" for games of chance, but they could not themselves play, however, they certainly played in private games. Play began at one half hour after sunset (from the first ringing of the Angelus) and continued to the twenty-third hour (changing seasonally).

At the entrance to the Ridotto was the *camera lunga*, or "long room" (twenty-two meters long by ten meters wide), with columns and railings in the gallery where the public could meet and chat while taking refreshments; cold drinks, coffee, pastries, cheese, wine, cold cuts, and fruit, was served in two adjacent rooms. Along the sides of the *camera lunga* were the first tables (called *tagliatori*) where

[3] *Letters d'Italie du Président de Brosses* (1739), p. 538.
[4] The inscription of the plaque read: *Giochi d'azzardo permessi tra le due colonne in piazzetta San Marco* (Games of chance permitted between two columns in the piazza of San Marco).
[5] The same fear motivated another rule whereby patricians were forbidden the slightest contact with foreigners, especially foreign envoys. *Memoires de L'ambassador FranÁois Joachim de Pierre de Bernis* (French Ambassador to Venice).
[6] The game of *giuoco delle biglie*, or 'game of marbles', the ancestor of our pinball machine, were also played in the ridotti or in taverns.

Johann Heinrich Tischbein, *Giocatori al Ridotto*, mid-18th Century, oil on canvas, 108.6 x 194.9 cm. Galerie Neuse, Bremen

croupiers shuffled the cards. In the next ten rooms which opened onto this *salone*, the atmosphere was intense and concentrated, far from the sociability taking place in the *camera lunga*. The deluxe setting contributed to the international fame and notoriety of the Ridotto.

Venice's greatest playwright, Carlo Goldoni described the atmosphere of the Ridotto:

> The famous *Ridotto* where all the gambling games had been permitted to the benefit of some and the ruin of others, attracting gamblers from all parts of the world, causing money to circulate. But it was a good idea to suppress this dangerous pastime, the *malafede* of certain players and the tricks of those who were the bankers in a city of 200,000 souls. The Republic of Venice recently prohibited gambling games and closed the *Ridotto*; perhaps private citizens could lament the closing, but there are those in the Gran Consiglio who loved gaming but still voted for the new decree.[7]

In his comedy *Le Donne Gelose* (The Jealous Women), Goldoni wrote of one room reserved exclusively for backgammon which he called *ai baraini*.

In 1768, after one hundred thirty years of continuous operation, the public Ridotto needed restoration. Ber-

[7]   Carlo Goldoni, *Memoirs* (1787).

nardino Maccaruzzi, the architect, was given the contract to modify the interior and make it more functional. Jacopo Guarana was hired to decorate the walls with frescoes. Funding was provided by the sale of properties of various monasteries and convents.

In 1774 the Venetian *Consiglio del Dieci* decreed the closing of the Ridotto (to the protestations of many). The *palazzo* which housed the Ridotto was occupied by the government magistrate and also used for storage. For a brief period during the French occupation, the palazzo reverted to its former function, only to be closed again during the Austrian occupation. It was used for festivities during the Carnival, and eventually restored and transformed in 1931 into a movie theater. The building had been the scene of the most intense gambling during the seventeenth and early-eighteenth centuries, more than all the Venetian salons and *casini* combined.

Cecilia, the wife of the great Venetian painter Giambattista Tiepolo (1696-1770), mother of his nine children and sister of the painter Francesco Guardi, was a frequent visitor to the Ridotto. She was said to have wagered her husband's drawings and their house in Zianigo while gambling. One night a collector won Tiepolo's sketches in a gamble she lost. She then wagered against their house on the mainland with its frescoes—Tiepolo had covered the walls of his country house with frescoes featuring the triumph of Punchinello—and again she lost. This happened while Tiepolo was away in Madrid. Fortunately, Tiepolo's son Domenico returned from Spain a few days later and was able to sort the matter out, but not without giving a large quantity of his father's drawings to the collector.[8]

Venetian ladies had their personal *ridotti*, either in small buildings apart from their family palaces or on the palace's mezzanine floor. There, they received friends, perhaps sipping hot chocolate and eating pastries, while playing cards. These buildings were also called *casini*. Many houses were sublet for gaming. One landlady, Paolina Marchi, owned twelve casini which she rented.

Gaming was the ubiquitous social activity of the inhabitants of the *palazzi*. The smaller *casino* was a more intimate (and easier to heat) gambling place than the ridotti. These were usually beautifully decorated, often with fres-

[8] This is probably the correct story of how the drawings passed from Tiepolo's studio to the Algarotti Corniani family and into the art market. Roberto Calasso, *Il Rosa Tiepolo*, Adelphi Editions: Milan, 2006.

Giuoco delle Biglie from Venice. Private collection

coes and stuccowork by renowned artists, and expensively furnished with mirrors, silver, Chinese porcelain, and fine paintings. Patricians ate, drank, and conversed at length, usually concluding their evenings with a game of *farone* or *bassetta* (public ridotti were less comfortable for players of farone) far from the prying eyes of servants.

By contrast, among the punishments for gambling suffered by the general populace were being put into a pillory and imprisonment for six years, for a first offense. The second offense mandated the nose and ears of the offender cut off and doubled the prison time. These punishments were, however, rarely enforced and, in any case, did little to prevent gambling.

The nature of play made *bassetta* more like a lottery than a card game. *Bassetta* (*bassette* in France) is played with four players; a banker and three players using a deck of fifty-two cards with French markings. The banker dealt thirteen covered cards to each of the players and themselves, then took two cards face down, one to the left and one to the right. Two sums of money were placed on the two cards leaving the rest covered in the center. Those on the left were winners for the banker, those to the right for the players. Then the players chose two cards and it was the turn of the players to pay up.

Tourists such as Francis Misson (*ca.* 1650-1722), remarked on the prevalence of gambling in Venice:

Lottery games in Venice were as widely practiced as were condemned when the Venetians developed their well-known public gaming rooms, the *Ridotto*; bets were also being taken again by specialist agents in the Rialto. The places which they call *Ridotti* are properly academies of *Basset*; they are open'd at the same time as the theatres and there are none but Noblemen who keep the Bank—they dismiss the Gamesters when they please and they have so much good fortune joyn'd to their privileges and skill, that the Bank is always the winner. There are ten or twelve chambers on a floor, with gaming tables in all of them. You can scarcely turn yourself in them; but tho' the throng is so great, yet there is always a profound silence. None are permitted to enter these places without masks.[9]

The games of the noble classes of the eighteenth century continued at their *terra ferma* (mainland properties),

[9]   Francis Misson, *A New Voyage to Italy with Curious Observations on Several Other Countries* (London, 1714).

Venetian Louis XVI Jeu de Loto Boards, circa 1775.
Courtesy Pelham Gallery

palazzi, and country villas. The Forsetti Villa in Santa Maria di Sala, for example, had fifteen tables distributed in ten rooms for gaming. By 1797 one hundred thirty-six private casini were in existence. The public *lotto* directed by the state also continued. Still, there had been a depression in Venice for some time, and this was the beginning of the end of the life of pleasure there!

Macca, a new game to Venice, became fashionable in 1787, but since it was determined to be a gambling game, it was subsequently officially banned. Nevertheless, it continued to be played in the private ridotti, in *caffè, piazze,* and *osterie* (simple eating and drinking places). Informal gambling sometimes took place in shop interiors (barbershops, hairdressers, and salons were known to harbor gamblers in their back rooms). The first coffee shop had opened in 1683, and, besides drinking coffee and gambling, discussions of literature, philosophy, and politics took place. Thirty-four caffés around Piazza San Marco had rooms often reserved for games on the upper floor.

In France, lotteries had been popular since the reign of Louis XIV and the *Régence.* Louis XV, his great-grandson and successor, saw the advantages of this sort of distraction. He instituted a royal lottery to replenish the coffers of the *École Militaire.* This was the last lottery run by the French state.

The game of lotto was particularly popular with the French royal family. As Baroness d'Oberkirch noted, the game of lotto was frequently played at Versailles: "At six o'clock at Versailles the game of lotto was played by *Mesdames* in Madame Adelaide's apartment, often the princes and princesses assisted in this game, it was always lotto".[10] Regarding an evening of especially excessive gambling at Versailles, the Baroness remarked, "Those who lost money wring my heart. What a humble and deadly passion! We returned to Paris at 3:30 in the morning!".[11] And further:

We were playing *lotto Dauphin*. The Duchesse de Villeroi mocked us amusingly regarding this game, it was very much in style and it really did not demand any work of intelligence. The princess Montbeliard in Alsace organized a lottery to benefit the poor. They were told to choose their numbers and that they would be promised a thousand things. The first twenty numbers in the *lotto* were the favorites. Everyone was excited and their faces were a study in gaiety and seriousness. The prince was not involved; he played chess in a corner with the Prince Abbot of Murbach.[12]

Madame d'Oberkirch quoted admonitory verses on the same subject by M. de Segur (which had been originally addressed to Madame de Luxembourg):

Le loto, quoi que l'on en dise,	Lotto whatever one says,
Sera fort longtemps en crédit;	Will be strong for a longtime on credit
C'est l'excuse de la bêtise	This is the excuse for the folly
Et le repos des gens d'esprit.	And the relaxation of people of intelligence
Ce jeu vraiment philosophique	This game is really philosophic
Met tout le monde de niveau ;	Puts everyone on a level
L'amour-propre si despotique	Self-love so despotic
Dépose son sceptre au loto.	Drops its sceptre to lotto
Esprit, bon goût, grâce et saillie,	Intelligence, good taste, grace and divine wit
Seront nuls tant qu'on y jouera.	Will be nothing while one plays it
Luxembourg, quelle modestie,	Luxembourg, what modesty
Quoi! Vous jouez à ce jeu-là !	What! You play that game there![13]

[10] *Mémoires de la Baronne d'Oberkirch.* Mercure de France (1989). A similar game was called *jeu de marelle* or "game of tokens".

[11] *Mémoires de la Baronne d'Oberkirch.* Mercure de France, 27 February 1785 (1989), p. 597.

[12] *Mémoires de la Baronne d'Oberkirch.* Mercure de France (1989), p. 219.

[13] *Mémoires de la Baronne d'Oberkirch.* Mercure de France (1989).

The English aristocracy was equally susceptible to the pleasures of the gaming table. It was in this context that the sandwich was developed, it is said, by the fourth Earl of Sandwich, as a convenient food, allowing eating and gambling simultaneously. In England, as in France, gambling had its addicts. In one case, the Duchess of Devonshire was forced to borrow from her friends in order to hide her losses from her husband. These debts "were so enormous as to create a dark cloud that plagued her most of her life. Despite her many attempts to quit, as her mother, Countess Spencer, had urged her to do, she continued to gamble".[14]

During the long winters in eighteenth century France, games of chance were also played on in bourgeois and artisans' houses and in hidden gardens; *brelan* and *lansquenet* tables attracted the money of the young bourgeoisie as well as craftsmen. Gaming popped up again as quickly as the authorities could stamp it out. In the midst of the Carnival in 1769 an anonymous letter denounced local gaming to the councils:

> It is shameful for an honest man to write an anonymous letter, but I am forced to do so in spite of myself for fear that otherwise some harm might befall me. As a father I am pleased to beg you to put an end to a game of chance that has long existed in my town. My children are ruining me, to say nothing of other families that have also been ruined. The guilty party is Sieur Balado, a stranger to these parts, who was driven out of Pamiers for having operated a card game there. He has a house near the Franciscans which is used only for gambling. I know that M. Andrieu (the first consul) has warned him not to operate that game, but in spite of that he continues to do so night and day. This is a scandalous thing near a church—from which they can be heard shouting and fighting.

The *habitués* of the gambling dens were reportedly driven to robbery. Raids were ineffective: "when the authorities were to enter, the lights were doused within, and in the darkness the gamblers smashed the lanterns carried by the consuls and their lackeys, allowing the players to flee".

About gambling in the French provinces, Jean-Franàois Marmontel (1723-1799) wrote of a fatal game of dice (*lansquenet*) played in Bordeaux, "with furor blackening the players' minds and absorbing their souls". He described his daily chagrin watching those who lost and were upset: "Their bitter cupidity", he said, combined with delight and their "social affectations" were "monstrous".

[14] "If we can keep her out of the fire for a year or two, or rather from being burned, for in the fire she is". Amanda Foreman. *Georgiana: Duchess of Devonshire* (New York: Random House, 2001), p. 36.

Madame Liselotte, the former German princess reported that at Versailles, "one plays here for frightening sums of money and the players seem without their senses".[15] They would, she added, "yell, then hit the tables with their fists that all the room can hear". Even the furniture suffered from a bad player!

Louis XV's queen, Marie Leszczynska (1703-1768), regularly organized games in her rooms; la cavagnole, *papillo*, and pharaon which were all equally popular with her ladies, and the betting was heavy.[16] The king's mistress, Madame de Pompadour (1721-1764), persuaded the king to pay off the 40,000 *écus* of gambling debts incurred by the queen in order, it was said, to keep herself in the queen's and the court's favor. Madame de Pompadour waited patiently while the king played a ritual game of cards with his wife in the evenings and sat through the king's nightly gambling parties before finally joined in herself.

The Paris parliament of the eighteenth century deplored the popularity of gambling in good society. They lamented their inability to punish this vice which threat-

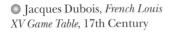 Jacques Dubois, *French Louis XV Game Table*, 17th Century

[15] "On joue ici des sommes effayantes et les joueurs sont comme des insensès". *Les Memoires de Liselotte Princesse Palatine.*
[16] The game continued in popularity. In a letter from Angelique de Bombelles (an intimate friend of Marie Antoinette) to her husband: *à sept heures nous faisons une grande toilette pour aller au salon où l'on arrive à sept heures trois quarts. On joue au pharaon jusqu'à dix heures. Apres on soupe. Apres le souper on se remer au pharaon qui dure jusqu'à je ne sais quelle heure!* ("[a]t seven at night we made our 'great toilette' to go to the salon at 7:45. We play *pharaon* until ten at night. Then, we have supper. After supper we go back to playing *pharaon*, which lasts until I don't know what time!").

● *Triple Top Game Table* from Germany, mid-18th Century

ened many families with ruin. While grim and silent in public, in private Louis XV was a lover of cards (as well as cats, preserves, prints, and coffee) it was said!

The French naturalist and mathematician, Comte de Buffon (1707-1788) remarked that gambling, for the aristocracy was "a passion so avid that the habit became [their] ruin". In Paris, the Duchesse de Praslin "received" every Monday to play a brelan for five people. The Comte de Cheverny wrote: that "up until three in the morning the street burned with the same fever". He also described Monseigneur Belsunce, of Marseille, "greatly winning, who tore at the cards with his front teeth, eyes bulging out of his face, and with a ferocious air that presaged something sinister". Here was another "uncool" player!

Another impassioned devotee, the Marquise du Ch,telet, despite being a scientist and intellectual, had to be bailed out repeatedly by her lover, Voltaire. She was especially addicted to *la cavagnole*, at which she usually lost. Toward the end of her life, her gambling losses exceeded her fortune.

In his memoirs, Prince Charles-Joseph de Ligne (1735-1814) warned of the dangers of gambling, referring to his own experiences:

After going on a hunt with the old Duc d'Orléans, I was tired and half asleep, and I won thirty thousand *ducats* and couldn't really wake up until an old lady who bet thirty or forty pulled my arm to pay her an *écu* of six francs which she cheated me! But thrown by this success into great adventures of gambling, I lost double what I had won and, after having played a game of eight thousand *ducats*, I finished the evening by losing seven thousand. I quit forever this most stupid of pleasures.[17]

He did not have much luck. The Prince de Ligne describes winning four or five hundred *ducats* before the battle of Brescal from the Polish General Wrbna, Count Desoffi, and three other officers. Then his luck turned: "I lost two thousand against Rodeny, Tomasoly, Gablosson, and Blankenstein, who is still alive. I asked the next day how these gentlemen were. Those who owed me money had been killed, and those I owed were all fine! One would say gold is my mortal enemy and it leaves me so that I am not tormented".[18]

Marie Antoinette was known as an extravagant game-player and gambler. Before spending her evenings in Madame de Polignac's company, she would occasionally spend the evening with the Duc and Duchesse de Duras, where a very bright young group gathered for what they called little games with questions; the *guerre-panpan*, *le colin-maillard*, and another called *des capativos*. The upper classes in Paris, always critical but nevertheless constantly imitating the ways of the court, also played these light social games. The governess of the *enfants de France*, Madame de Guérnénee, received a brilliant society who gambled in her salon. In her *Mémoires* Madame Campan described the atmosphere of gaming at *Chateau* Marly:

To be admitted to the game of the Queen for an evening at Marly, it sufficed to be a well-dressed man nominated and presented by an officer of the court, to be given the right to play in the game room. The *salon* was of very large octagonal form, and the room was raised to an Italian style roof which terminated in a cupola ornamented with balconies where ladies, not presented, were able to enjoy the view of this brilliant gathering. The rich and

[17] *Mémoires du Prince de Ligne*, Cahier V, Mercure de France (2004).
[18] *Mémoires du Prince de Ligne*, Cahier XII. Mercure de France (2004).

the heavy bettors of Paris never missed an evening at the *salon* of the Marly *château* and the sums won or lost were always considerable. Louis XVI detested heavy gambling and was in bad humor when told of their large losses.[19]

Marie-Antoinette's reputation suffered considerably from her enthusiasm for gambling. According to Madame Campan, Emperor Joseph II, brother of Marie Antoinette, accused Marie Antoinette of having a "real gambling den—*un vrai tripot*" at Versailles. We are given some insight by the Countess de Boigne:

> The Count d'Artois and the queen played a game with stakes so enormous that they were obliged to admit that they had to find all the degenerates of Europe to play with them. It was of this unhappy passion from which sprang the slanders that flooded the life of this unhappy queen with such a quantity of troubles, even before the historic unhappiness began for her. When one plays, one wishes to win, and it is impossible to avoid the appearance of greediness. The princes, accustomed to everything going their way, were almost always poor players, and it was one reason more for them to avoid heavy betting. But if the queen didn't love the game, why did she play? She played because of another of her passions; she played to be in style and above all she wanted to be *à la mode*. She incurred debt to flirtatiously be so in style. To be a pretty woman and the most *à la mode*, was the title she most desired.[20]

Though gambling was eventually banned from the palace, even in their last horrible months before the monarchy's collapse, the royal family continued to play cards. Two days after the fall of the Bastille in 1789, the general populace still played the royal lottery.

Gaming in Paris was vividly described by Président de Brosses, counselor of the Parliament de Bourgogne in his *Voyage en Italie* (1739): "The handsome exterior of the *hôtel* formerly belonging to the Princess de Carignan . . . belied the fact that it had become a gambling rendezvous. On the ground floor, billiards was played in the *brelan* (or gambling den) as it was in the *hôtel* belonging to the Duchesse de Maine. The *lansquenet* excited the players because the out-

[19] Marly was built by Louis XIV eight kilometers from Versailles, it was composed of a central pavilion—called the King's pavilion—surrounded by twelve other pavilions with an allusion to the king's emblem the sun and the twelve zodiac signs. Marly became a favorite retreat from Versailles for Louis XV, where the etiquette was less severe than at Versailles. The king carefully selected his guests as they caused considerable expense. *Mémoires de Madame Campan, Première femme de chambre de Marie Antoinette.* Mercure de France. p. 541, pp. 232-233.

[20] *Mémoires de la Comtesse de Boigne I Du regne de Louis XVI à 1820.* Mercure de France (1999).

Venetian "arte povera" game box, with four smaller boxes and counting chips, ca. 1725-35. Private Collection

come of the entire game rested on the appearance of only one card". The Duchesse de Maine was famous for her wild gambling. She was known to have lost a fortune but continued to play nevertheless. *Tric-trac*, or backgammon, was also being played, but, according to de Brosses, "probably by non-Parisians, as it was a tamer game and was played in a corner of the room". The attitude of the fashionable gentlemen, continued Président de Brosses, "was to seem unaffected by either winning or losing".

Not long before the French Revolution, the Count de Genlis ran a gambling house in Place Vendôme. The young Count Alexandre de Tilly recounted in his memoirs that he had never liked gambling but, "joined the players of good company there, and a few who were not". M. de Genlis warned de Tilly to "amuse himself, have supper, but hold on to his money", but de Tilly wrote, "the occasion was present and stronger than Genlis' eloquence". After visiting another well known gambling house where "men and women of all ages, social ranking, and color" were received, de Tilly was criticized by his relatives. De Tilly also witnessed M. de

● Gaetano Renoldi, *Card Table with Folding Top*, late 18th Century

Montesquieu, who was still involved in the kingdom's public finances, lose immense sums amounting to 100,000.00 *écus* in a single night. De Montesquieu would only leave the gambling place in the morning to go directly to the assembly to report on the finances of the state.

According to de Tilly gambling houses in London were dismal, "antechambers of hell . . . with such a trap on every street for inexperience and avidity. They were more deadly and dangerous than those of Paris. Drunkenness, the dominant vice of the English nation, created hardier knaves and more docile victims".

In the eighteenth century gambling in France broke down some of the rigid social hierarchies that existed among the upper classes. The same enthusiasm for gambling brought princes of the blood, like the Comte d'Artois, Louis XVI's brother and the future Charles X, to the same table as those with no titles at all. These changes in social behavior were remarked upon by Charles Maurice de Talleyrand (1754-1815):

Gambling and the *bel esprit* had leveled everything. Careers, the great supporters of hierarchy and of order, were being destroyed. All young men considered themselves fit to govern. All ministerial action was criticized. What the king and the queen did personally was subjected to discussion and nearly always met with the disapproval of the Paris *salons*. Young women spoke pertinently about all aspects of the administration.[21]

De Talleyrand was himself reproached for his addiction to cards about 1805, to which he quipped: "you do not play then at whist, sir? Alas, what a sad old age you are preparing for yourself".[22]

Gaming in social settings continued after Revolution. In 1803, the fifteen-year-old Arthur Schopenhauer in *Journal de Voyage* wrote of Bordeaux during Carnival that "all people flocked to the *Grand Théâtre*, where admission was only three *livres*", he continued:

The principal distraction at these masked balls was gambling. A series of tables in the long rooms provided a ready surface for such distraction; there were tables one could rent for 12 *livres*, at which each had one or two people occupied with dominoes plus others not masked, including women. The women had next to them an enormous pile of fake *louis* of gold and who, tapping on the tables with the coins, incited the people to play at dice with them at whatever amount of money, as low as a gold *louis*. Generally the women won, as many gave their good *louis* against the fake ones, there was also a table to make exchanges, where the players would give five fake gold *louis* for two real ones. In another *salle*, revelers played roulette.[23]

[21] *Mémoires de Talleyrand*, quoted in Benedetta Craveri, *The Age of Conversation* (New York: New York Review of Books, 2005), p. 373.
[22] *Vous ne jouez donc pas le whist, Monsieur? Hélas! Quelle triste viellesse vous vous préparez. Mémoires de Talleyrand* (1816).

Lord Granville, the British ambassador to Paris in 1816, was known in Paris as *Le Wellington des Joueurs* for his addiction to gaming. He lost 23,000 *écus* once on a single night.[24] Some of the games required mental agility, a varying combination of psychological reasoning, speculation, concentration, and memory which, clearly, he must have lacked. Swiss-born novelist and politician Benjamin Constant (1767-1830), who pursued the novelist Madame de Staël (1766-1817), was a brilliant conversationalist but a wild gambler who came to her frequently for money when he lost. In 1785 a lady named Louisa Stewart wrote that the French ambassador "suffered a stroke of Palsy yesterday", yet guests went to his house anyway, "and played faro etc., as if he had not been dying in the next room. We are curious people".[25]

During the eighteenth century in Russia, gambling was so much a part of society that serfs could easily be bought and sold, whole families could be bartered against horses or hunting dogs or gambled away in a night of card play-

[23]   Mercure de France (1989).
[24]   Hugh Thomas, *The Slave Trade: the Story of the Atlantic Slave Trade, 1440-1870* (New York: Simon & Schuster, 1997), p. 538.
[25]   Bill Bryson, *At Home: A Short History of Private Life* (New York: Doubleday, 2010), p. 114.

ing. Princess Daschkoff of Russia related a game played with the Emperor of Russia:

> In this game [*campis*], each person has a certain number of chances and the survivor is he who wins. The stake that each player had thrown on the green rug was one of ten *impérials*, a sum much too exaggerated for my purse. Especially as the emperor, when he lost, pulled an *Impérial* from his pocket and threw it on the rug, a handy maneuver which would make him win. As soon as the game finished, the emperor proposed a second game where I prayed him to leave me out. He insisted that I play again, but I refused obstinately. Then he offered to go partners with me. I refused again, until finally I was obliged to declare, like a skinned child (as he treated me by habit as a child) that I was not rich enough to be cheated, but that I (he called me "her majesty") wished to play like everyone else, we could then have some chance. After his usual pleasantries he allowed my escape, everyone looked upon me with astonishment when I retreated from the circle and exclaimed 'that woman there has spirit!'.[26]

Gambling continued to consume Europe throughout the eighteenth and nineteenth centuries, amounting to a daily activity at the courts and the leisure classes.

⬤ *German Card Table*, mid-18th Century

[26] *Mémoires de Princesse Daschkoff, Dame d'honneur de Catherine II, Impératrice de toutes les Russies.* Mercure de France, pp. 52-53.

Black Figure Plate, *Warriors Playing
a Board Game*, ca. 520 B.C.

Board Games

By gaming we lose both time and treasure,
two things most precious to the life of man.
Owen Feltham, *Resolves,* 1623

The earliest games were placed in tombs in ancient civilizations to entertain the dead in the afterlife, such as in the Theban tomb of Queen Nefertari (who died in 1199 B.C.) in the Valley of the Queens. A wealth of archaeological finds in Scandinavia has produced a variety of evidence about board games, playing pieces, dice, and methods of play. Four checkered boards were found in a bog in Denmark dating from the Iron Age (approximately 1200 B.C.-400 A.D.) and three game boards were found in Lund, Scandinavia and in Uppakra, Denmark, along with eighteen gaming pieces—eight made of glass—found next to important buildings in the center of the settlement. Two hundred thirty-eight gaming items were found there made of bone, horn, or wooden disks. King Magnus of Denmark (r. 1042-1047) was known to have owned a large ivory chessboard. Cistercian monasteries built in Sweden in 1142 by royal initiative are also a rich source of gaming materials, as were many other monasteries. In Scandinavian societies, games previously thought to have been an exclusively male activity seem also to have been played by women and children.

The game *halatafl,* mentioned in the Gretlis Saga (ca. 1300 A.D.) evolved into the Fox and Geese "hunt" type of game; two players had an unequal number of pieces on a board with two sides. In the game, either the fox devoured the geese or the geese trapped the fox for victory. An early form of this game had a board with thirty-three holes arranged in a cross. References to the game are found in the household accounts of King Edward IV (r. 1442-1483) of England. There were versions of this game in Iceland, the Netherlands, Russia, and Nepal.

The French variant of Fox and Geese games was called *Le Renard et les poules* and had thirty-seven pieces rather than thirty-three. A later version had seventeen geese and did not permit movement backwards but eventually diagonal moves were permitted to address this limitation. A simpler version still exists which can be played with checkers—four geese and one fox—using diagonal moves. The geese aim to trap the fox, but they do not have backward movement.

Among "race games", *Mehen* was the name of the Egyptian version of the popular Asian board game Snakes.[1] One of the oldest mehen boards known bears the name of Ana, second king of the first dynasty from around 3000 B.C. The game is pictured in the tomb of a royal official named Hesy, found in Saggarah and dating from approximately 2650 B.C. The tomb also showed accessories for three games, mehen, *senet*, and *m'n* (which consisting of sixteen vertical lines or spaces in a row).

The "cross and circle" race game parcheesi (*pachisi*) is the Westernized version of a game indigenous to Ancient India. In American, Ludo (I play) is the simpler version of parcheesi. Many other games from France, Germany, and Spain for children have the cross and circle structure of the race game parcheesi. Played by four players in two teams, pachisi means 'twenty-five' because the board has four branches forming a cross of eight places each, which, when added to the central square make twenty-five. In an early version, the player's pieces move around the board according to the throw of six or seven sea snails (or cowry shells) distinguished by their color. The number of shells landing opening upwards indicated the number of moves allowed. The teams' objective was to move their pieces completely around the board counter-clockwise before their opponent could accomplish the feat. According to legend the sixteenth-century B.C. Indian Emperor Akbar I had a huge pachisi board of inlaid marble on pavement in the city of Fatehpier Sikkri where he used slaves as the pawns; sixteen young female slaves wearing specific colors moved about the red and white squares as directed by the throws of the cowry shells.

One version of parcheesi was played in the Middle East

[1] This game is not to be confused with today's Snakes and Ladders, a game popular at the end of the nineteenth century and still played today.

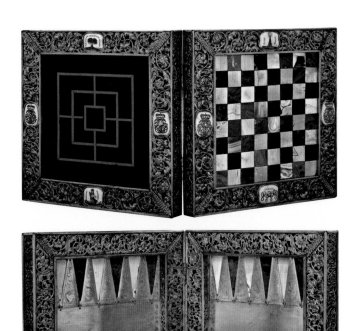

German Gameboard Box, before 1683, boxwood and gilded metal and enamel

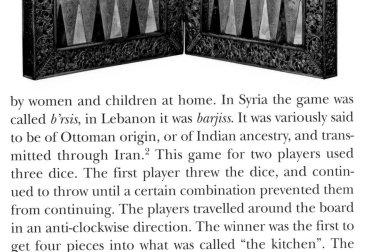

by women and children at home. In Syria the game was called *b'rsis,* in Lebanon it was *barjiss.* It was variously said to be of Ottoman origin, or of Indian ancestry, and transmitted through Iran.[2] This game for two players used three dice. The first player threw the dice, and continued to throw until a certain combination prevented them from continuing. The players travelled around the board in an anti-clockwise direction. The winner was the first to get four pieces into what was called "the kitchen". The dice were broken shells with lead or copper poured into the oval openings and the edges smoothed over.

The fifteenth-century Aztec Emperor Montezuma watched his nobles playing a game like parchisi called *patolli.* Here, the board was a squared off, diagonally-placed, cross. The players walked with the patolliztli mat rolled under their arms and carried a basket with markers of colored stones (precious stones, fine turquoise, and gold beads). They placed an offering of food in a fire bowl filled with incense in the hope that the dice would be

[2]   An Iranian game board made of wood is at the Golestan Palace Museum in Teheran. Thanks to Dr. Irving Finkel of the British Museum for this information.

favorable as they played for high stakes. The players invoked the god Macullxocriti by rubbing five beans between their hands, shouting the god's name, and tossing the beans to a mat. Instructions for the game and scoring rules were recorded in a sixteenth-century book by father Diego Duran, a book that was suppressed by ecclesiastical authorities for over 300 years before being published in Mexico as *Historia de las Indias de Nueva-España & Islas de Tieira Firme* in 1867.

Popular seventeenth and eighteenth-century Italian board games included *Gioco de l'Oca* (Game of the Goose), *Gioco del Barone* (Baron's game), and rustic games such as *Gioco degli asini* (Game of the donkeys), *Gioco dei Nasi* (Illustrating Noses), *Gioco della gola* (Gluttons Around a Table), *Gioco della barca* (Game of the Ship), *Gioco Romano o della piotta* (Roman game of the Pious), *Gioco del Tarocco* (Tarot Game) and *Gioco del Biribisse. Gioco reale* (Royal Game of Backgammon) popular in eighteenth-century

● Charles Nicolas Cochin II,
Games of the King and Queen in the Hall of Mirrors at Versailles,
18th Century, engraving.
Grand Palais, Paris

THE HISTORY AND DEVELOPMENT OF SPECIFIC GAMES

Venice, was a game in which the players, as in lotto or bingo, extracted winning numbers. *Gioco reale* had eighty squares on a board or painted canvas that featured animals, people, flowers, and fruit as well as allegorical figures such as Fortune and Justice. In Tuscany during the eighteenth century, dice were used in conjunction with game boards similar to those used for checkers or chess. *Tavola reale, gioco dell'oca*, and *sbaraglino* were played with dice which determined the moves.

The racing game *Giuoco del'oca* called *jeu de l'oie* in France, traces it origins to ancient Greece. It is a game of chance, played with dice and is distinctive for having inspired a variety of thematic illustrations and editions. It came into prominence in Europe at the end of the sixteenth century with the prevailing taste for Hellenism. Famously, Francesco I de Medici, Grand Duke of Tuscany (1574-1587) sent King Philip of Spain a gift of a *Giuoco de l'Oca*.

The *jeu de l'oie* was very popular in seventeenth-century France. The earliest extant French game was made in Lyon in 1601. The doctor of the infant Louis XIII wrote in his diary that when Louis was two years old he liked playing the game. An early version from the Dietsch Collection at the Palais du Roi de Rome (in Rambouillet near Paris) called the *jeu du monde* or Game of the World—reissued in 1659 by the geographer Pierre Duval—had a geography theme. Other editions included one on the buildings and monuments of Paris. One *jeu de l'oie* from 1661, engraved by De Voullemont, was scientifically focused, with illustrations of plants and the discoveries and inventions of the ages. Another example from 1705, now in the Palais du Roi du Rome, has small engravings with the qualities, faults, and vices of society. Also at Rambouillet, a *jeu de l'oie* called *Marie-claire*, designed by Beauville, has forty-nine examples of the life and activities of women. The *jeu de l'oie* could also be used for religious purposes, some games were created by the church hierarchy and destined for heretics, but some religious games played with dice were thought unfit for convents. An English version of the game from 1780 featured French fashions, hairstyles, hats, and poufs of the period.

Chocolate was an indispensable stimulant in the high

● *Gueridon circular table*, ca. 1780, mahogany and mahogany veneer, mouldings of brass and plaques of striped bronze, inset white marble top

● Jean-Jacques Pafrat, *Bouillotte table*, ca. 1785. Oak and pine wood, inlaid with lemon wood, amaranthine and ebony, gilded bronze, brass and leather

French Bouillotte lamp, ca. 1790, gilded bronze and painted metal *tôle*. Private Collection

ranking *salon du jeu*. It was eaten as candy or enjoyed as hot chocolate. The stimulant must have functioned to keep the players awake as the game extended far into the night! The Marquise de Châtelet once played thirty-three hours nonstop, hard work but the chocolate must have helped. Silver chocolate pots far outnumbered tea and coffee pots in eighteenth century France.

Gaming required specialized furniture, tables and chairs were especially made for gaming and gambling in France, Germany, and Italy. In France there were chairs named *voyeuse ponteuse* (from the verb *ponter,* meaning "placing one's bets") and *flamandes* (Flemish). The *délassant* (relaxing) chair permitted the player to follow the

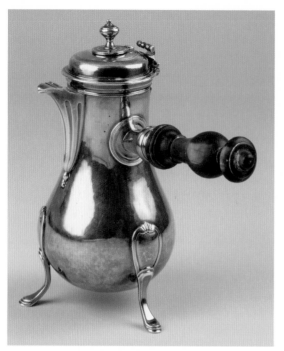

● Jan Nicholas Saget, *Chocolatière*, 1798, silver and wood, 22 x 12 cm. Private Collection

● *Chocolatière*, 18th Century, silver and wood. Private Collection

● *Louis XV Voyeuse Chairs,*
18th Century

● *German Table a Jeux,* mid-18th Century

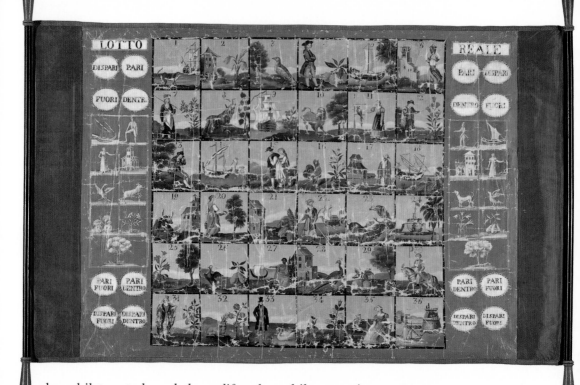

play whilst seated, and the *califourchon* while squatting. The *voyeuse* (observer) was more convenient than a regular chair for ladies as it accommodated their style of dress Another type, a *voyeuse* with a higher seat, could be used sitting facing forward or backward and the high upholstered end could be leaned upon by another observer of the game. Alternatively, the player could also put his knees on the seat and lean forward with his forearms placed on the upholstered top of the back. The closed sided armchair, called a *bergère* (a wing chair) could also be made in the *voyeuse* style. Some of these chairs were designed to hold a small box for cards and chips. The artists and artisans in France and Italy were always aware that comfort and convenience were important to their clientele and this ever-gambling leisure class were the chair-makers' steady customers. Writing tables, dressing tables, and the ubiquitous card table were all portable in order to be placed where desired and to be easily moved.

Furniture makers working in the *Bonne-Nouvelle* quarter of Paris, called *menuisiers*, obligingly made a specialty of these chair types, included famous manufacturers such as Bovo, Delanois, Gourdin, Jacob, Avisse, Boulard, Sené,

● *Venetian Gioco Reale*, mid-18th Century. Private Collection

● *Biribi Games Table* from Northern Italy, ca. 1790-1810, pear wood with inlaid ebony. Private Collection

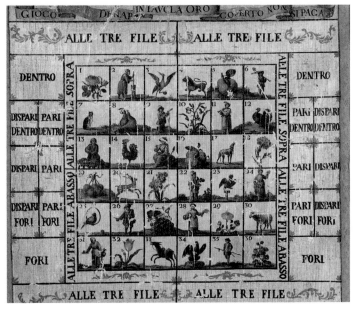

Tilliard, and Pluvinet. The Cresson, Gourdin, and Foliot families were especially active in producing these items. Foliot supplied the Crown until 1786 and the Jacob family continued production well into the nineteenth century. The work of the *menuisiers* followed the evolution of furniture styles from the early eighteenth century through the Revolution and beyond.

In 1866 a lithographer from Massachusetts named Milton Bradley produced *The Checkerboard Game of Life,* this board game had squares representing life events from infancy to old age. The playing board was inspired by the checkerboard but was a game of chance as the player moved along the board by means of a top or small spinning wheel. The modern version of the game, now called The Game of Life, is still popular in the United States. This kind of board game, played without dice or cards which had been tainted by association with gambling, was much more family-friendly and paved the way for family entertainment games such as Monopoly and Scrabble which were first produced in 1933 and 1938, respectively.

Monopoly is a game for multiple players represented by tokens who move along the board with the aid of dice, acquiring "properties". The winner amasses the most properties or holds the most "cash". The original goal of the game created by a Washington, D.C. feminist named Lizzie Maqie in 1903, however, was quite the opposite. Initially called The Landlord's Game it critiqued corporate America, the evils of monopolization, and the titans of the age, such as Andrew Carnegie, J.P. Morgan, and John D. Rockefeller. There were two sets of rules: one in which the object was to get rich quickly, the other where all players benefitted from the wealth created. The get-rich-quickly rules were the more popular (as one could imagine)!

Charles Darrow sold the concept to Parker Brothers who marketed it in 1935 in the now familiar version. An anti-Monopoly game in the 1970s returned the game to its earlier liberal roots following a ten-year lawsuit in which the Supreme Court debated whether Parker Brothers had illegally monopolized "Monopoly". Eventually a settlement granted the founder of the anti-Monopoly game, Ralph Anspach, the right to sell his game. Twenty-first century

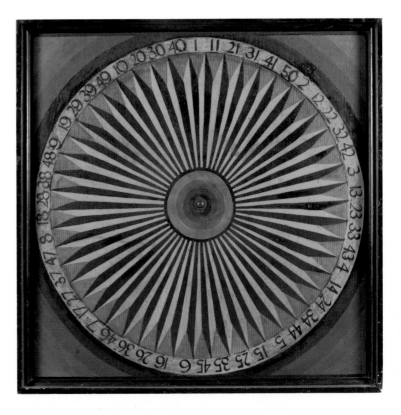

American Carnival Arcade Target, ca. 1900. Private Collection

players can play Monopoly Empire, which substitutes traditional property names with those of well-known corporations such as Coca Cola, Nestle, and McDonald's. In this version players acquire brands to create corporate empires and the new tokens are a Corvette, an Xbox controller and a Paramount Pictures movie clapboard. There are currently several digital versions of Monopoly.

Clue is another well-known modern board game. A British game from 1949 called Cluedo inspired Clue, and it was initially controversial because it featured particularly menacing weapons such as hypodermic needles and a poison bottle as tokens and included a character called Reverend Green who could potentially be accused of murder.

Naturally, board games have migrated on-line, for example *The Sims* is a video and computer game released in 2000, which has generated more than four billion dollars. In this game there are no moves or goals, instead the player creates an on-line environment and personality, or avatar.

A Game of Backgammon, late 18th Century,
gouache, att. Giuseppe Bernardino Bison.
Private Collection

Backgammon

Man is a gaming animal. He must always be trying to get the better in something or other.
Charles Lamb, *Essays of Elia*, 1823

Backgammon is the oldest known board game. Like draughts (checkers) and chess, backgammon is a positional game; a game played on a board that has patterns and markings which define the movements of the pieces on the board in relation to each other. Boards were found in the Royal Tombs at Ur in Mesopotamia (now southern Iraq), excavated in the 1920s by Sir Leonard Woolley. The excavation produced five game boards made of wood, decorated with shell, lapis lazuli, red paste, and red limestone set into bitumen and decorated with rosettes and animals. The boards had white pieces engraved with animals, colored rosettes, seven black and seven white counters, and six dice in the forms of pyramids dotted with inlay. Each player seems to have had six dice and seven men. The moves were made by casting the pyramided dice, and the aim was to get one's pieces into position on the board. In another area, archaeologists found simpler boards with two sets of black squares inlaid with five lapis dots and others where shell squares were engraved with vignettes. Ur dwellers had access by river and canal to the Persian Gulf, where backgammon could have spread to the west from about 3000 B.C. A board dating from ca. 1580 B.C. with similarities to the Ur board was found in Cyprus. It is also possible that backgammon may have originated in Kerman (Iran), where the boards had three lines of twelve counters.

Senat is the Egyptian forerunner of the backgammon family of games. Egyptian boards seem to have developed from those at Ur—with box-shaped boards similar to those at Ur, usually 32 x 15" wide (81 x 38 cm)—and a drawer to hold the counters and dice. In Tutankhamen's tomb in the Nile Valley, there was a board on which Queen Hatshepsut's name was inscribed, as well as lion-headed pieces, an ancient symbol of power. With the discovery of the Egyptian Qustul tombs (during works raising the level of the Aswan Dam) an elaborate game was found under a leather bag containing fifteen ivory and fifteen ebony game pieces, and five cube-shaped ivory dice within a box. The die were supposed to be dropped through the open top onto a grooved, inclined, board where they die turned and rolled out of the bottom between two carved dolphins.[1] Similar dice boxes were used until the fifth century A.D. in the Greco-Roman world to prevent cheating.

⬤ *Roman Game Board,* 2nd Century B.C.

In the sixth century A.D., Greeks played a game known as *tabla* or *taula.* Plato mentions a form of the game, played for money, and commented on its popularity. The Greeks had a game called *kubera,* also known as *grammar.* These games were often built like boxes, which held counters, and might include another game on the underside, such as the game known as thirty squares. It was adapted by the Romans in the first century and said to have been played by the soldiers on the Roman frontiers. A marble backgammon board from Late Antiquity, after the establishment of Christianity, featured a Greek cross carved in its middle and the inscription which read, "our Lord Jesus Christ grants aid and victory to dicers if they write His name when they role the dice".

The Roman game *Ludus Duodecim Scriptorum* (Twelve-lined Game), described by Ovid (43 B.C.-17/18 A.D.) in *The Art of Loving,* was probably derived from the Greek game.[2] It had a board with a line for each month of the year, and the thirty pieces (fifteen black and fifteen white) were moved with a throw of the dice. The Roman Emperor Claudius (41-54 A.D.) wrote a book about *tabula* (as did the Byzantine Emperor Zeno, four centuries later). By the sixth century, the game known as *alea,* had four parts of the board named "tables", which became the name of both the board and the game, *tabula,* as well as its variant which had only two rows of marked pieces.

Nero was said to have played tables for the modern equivalent of $15,000 a point. Emperor Commodus was accused of having turned the imperial palace into a gambling palace; he was said to have appropriated a large sum from the treasury, ostensibly to finance an expedition to the African

[1]   The Indian game of parcheesi may have been a remote ancestor.
[2]   The game had several names; one was *ludus duodecim scriptorium,* twelve-line game for the twelve points on either side of the board, and was played with three dice rather than two.

provinces, but he went back to the game and lost it all.

In Pompeii, there is a backgammon table depicted in two scenes of wall paintings; in one, two players are arguing about a game being played; in the second, the innkeeper is throwing out two players having a fight, showing that games were played by other than the elite.

The popularity of backgammon has been credited to King Ardashir, the Unifier (180-242 A.D.) the first Sasanian king. The present structure of the game harks back to Persia in the reign of King Ardashir (226-241 A.D.). The Persian name for backgammon, *narshir*, was mentioned in the Babylonian Talmud between 300-500 A.D. Still today, throughout the Middle East counting is in Persian whenever backgammon is played. The Chinese document the game *nard* (itself of Indian derivation) in the third century A.D., it was referred to as *t'shu-p'u'* in Sung manuscripts of 900-1229 A.D., and identified as the origin of backgammon. A similar game is called *shwan-lu* in China, in Japan it is *sunorokie*, in Korea, *ssang-ry-ouk*, in Thailand, *len sake* or *saka*, and in Malaysia, *main tabal.*

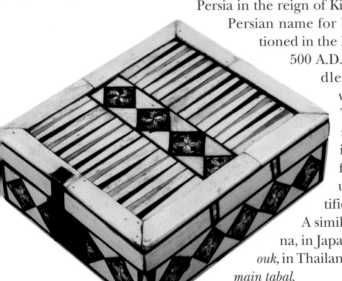

● *Venetian Game Box*, circa 1500, ivory and ebony. Private Collection

The Louvre in Paris has in its collection two backgammon boards on the reverse of ivory plaques from Gaul (possibly from central France) or Italy, dating from the fifth century A.D. The ivory plaques show two groups of apostles below a medallion of Christ. The backgammon game, incised on the back of the plaques, formed a complete table when both wings were joined. The ornamentation is of palmettes, geometric designs, and a braided motif.[3]

Another game of *tables* was excavated at Saint-Denis, in France, and is made of bone, iron, and wood. It was found one hundred meters north of the monastic complex that had been abandoned in the first quarter of the seventh century. Indeed, it was probably made even earlier, as ceramics found there attest to a very early date and origin.[4]

Counters for backgammon have also been excavated, along with chess pieces and the game called *mérelle. Mérelle*

[3] See *La France Romane* (Paris: Musée du Louvre, 2005).
[4] *Ibid.*, p. 196.

was a strategy board game for two players believed to have originated with Roman soldiers, similar to backgammon, with the difference that the board was empty at the beginning of the game. Two players held nine pieces each which were placed one at a time onto the board. Lots were drawn for the advantage of being first. The aim was to reduce the opponent to two pieces or to immobilize them. Emperor Claudius wrote a book about the game and had a table mounted on his chariot so that he could play while traveling. Domitian was cited as an expert player, and Caligula accused of cheating at the game.

Elsewhere, games similiar to tables were found in Troy and a Bronze Age site in Ireland where the game could have been introduced by Phoenician or Greek traders about 900 A.D. Backgammon counters are of two types; decorated with geometric decoration and those with figural motifs such as zodiac and bestiary subjects. Some were made of wood, others of bone. Traces of pigment have been found on some counters suggesting they would have been colored.

The boards for *tabulas*, from which backgammon or *trictrac* are derived, are found throughout the Middle Ages. The game was popular in medieval Europe; including a variant with twelve pieces which originated in the fourteenth century. Like chess, it was very popular from the tenth to twelfth centuries in France.

The players of chess were aristocrats and those of backgammon perhaps of a somewhat lower social level. Between the fifteenth and eighteenth centuries, backgammon became a fashionable pastime throughout Europe. A Venetian law of 1268 cites the game of *tabulas* and chess as the only games allowed by law. A backgammon board was part of an early inventory of a casino at the Giudecca, Venice, probably part of the usual casino equipment. The will of Pietro Vîlion, a Venetian trader in Tabriz (Persia), dating from about 1263, specified that amongst his possessions he owned gold, silver, pearl, and jasper jeweled chess and backgammon boards.[5]

In Venice—*una casetta nera de baraglin* was an old Venetian name for backgammon—boxes of bone or ivory, ebony, and walnut with patterns for playing backgammon and chess were common possessions of thirteenth and four-

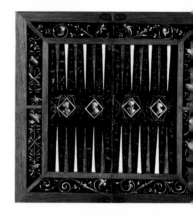

● Léonard Limousin, *Tric Trac Board*, 1537, enamel on copper, 46.5 x 47 cm. Musée du Louvre, Paris ML 128

[5]   Deborah Howard, from a lecture on Venice and Islam on March 29, 2007.

teenth century patricians. The Embriachi family workshop collected notable game boxes, ranging from the simple to the elaborate. Fourteenth to sixteenth century Venetian boxes (pictured here) have a backgammon board on the lid and a chessboard at the base, and are decorated with star-like designs *alla Certosina*.[6] Some of the boxes have iron carrying rings along their sides, hinges, a lock plate, and a clasp. The interior of some are lined with rusty-pink linen to cushion the counters.

Louis XIII Folding Backgammon Box, ebony and ivory. Private Collection

Backgammon was extremely popular in Florence where Niccolò Machiavelli (1469-1527) was known to play tric-trac in his leisure hours. Another notable devotee was Pope Julius II, the patron of Michelangelo's Sistine Chapel ceiling. One week after the pope was so ill that he received last rites, he recovered sufficiently to play tric-trac and listen to musicians.[7]

Professional backgammon players traveled around Europe in the seventeenth and eighteenth centuries and lived on proceeds from their games. Casanova described such a player in his *Mémoires*: "as for him, he lived on the game of tric-trac, although he had luck with dice, his ability in that game was of more value than luck".[8]

In Italy, and especially France, a new type of table made for playing backgammon was added to the furnishings of the fashionable interior, these game tables followed changes in furniture design from the Renaissance through the late-eighteenth century. In the eighteenth century makers of high quality tables in Paris (called *ébenistes* after their early use of expensive ebony wood) were established in Faubourg Saint-Antoine. At the time of Louis XV, aside from French born artisans, many parisian *ébenistes* originated from Italy and about a third of them came from the Lowlands. During the reigns of Louis XV and XVI, many *ébenistes* also came from Germany, and several veritable dynasties were formed. French-born artisans and some of the *ébenistes* of Dutch and German origin— including Bernard I van Risen Burgh

6   *Certosina* work is fifteenth-century Italian inlay work with polygonal tesserae of wood, bone, or metal or mother-of-pearl arranged in geometric pattern, from the Veneto and Lombardy in particular. It was originally inspired by Egyptian techniques from the ninth century.
7   Ross King, *Michelangelo and the Pope's Ceiling* (London: Penguin Books, 2003), p. 240.
8   Giacomo Casanova, *Mémoires, Volume II* (1789), pp. 650-664, p. 990.

(BVRB), Riesener, Latz, and others—sold their pieces as retailers along with furniture made by their colleagues. Due to their entry into the guild and taxes imposed on their works (it was the reason they signed their works, unless the objects were made for the court which precluded taxes being levied), much more is known about fine French eighteenth-century furniture than furniture from any other countries and periods.

In addition to portable game sets similar to modern ones, the most common surviving type is the popular rectangular neoclassic *tric-trac* table, which had a removable top and was lined on the underside with baize. Some had inlaid game boards on the surface while others had a board within the table and a leather surface edged in wood. The tables had drawers for counters and to hold the silver or gilt bronze candleholders that could have been set into the borders. Many examples of this type survive.

Louis XVI didn't often engage in the games that occupied his wife and the court, instead he played *tric-trac* and wagered only small sums. As he told one heavy better, "I

● Pascale Coignard, *Tric Trac Table* (*Table de jeu du Dauphin au Temple*), cabinetwork, felt, leather and wood. Private Collection

THE HISTORY AND DEVELOPMENT OF SPECIFIC GAMES

Mahogany Louis XVI backgammon table with leather inset top with candleholders on each end, tapered and fluted legs with sabots. Private Collection

understand that you play great games and that it amuses you; you play with money of your own, but I, I would be playing with the money of others".[9] A similar scruple was displayed by Emperor Joseph II, and critically relayed by Baronne d'Oberkirch:

> In the evening one played a strong little game, at least relatively, the emperor, questioned on his wisdom, rare in a sovereign, said that he felt scruples losing the money of his subjects. I found this a bit pretentious and that in everything he always posed, as if there were a moralist painting, the portrait of his virtues, behind him.[10]

A contemporary of Madame d'Oberkirch, Mme de Staël wrote that "[i]f it were not for games, nothing would happen at all . . . A hostess's principal care was to lure her guests to a *tric-trac* table as quickly as possible".[11] King Charles X of France (r. 1824-1830) owned a game of backgammon, where the counters were designed to illustrate his kinships and alliances, including a claimed descendance from the Biblical David.

[9] Charles de Brosses, *Lettres d'Italie du Président de Brosses.*
[10] *Mémoires de la baronne d'Oberkirch.* Presented by Suzanne Burkard. *Mercure De France* (1970-1989).
[11] De Staël, *Letters* (April, 1785).

Jean-Léon Gérôme, *Almehs Playing
Chess in a Café*, 1870, oil on canvas.
Private Collection

Chess

You cannot play at chess if you are kind hearted.
French Proverb

Although chess was well known in the first century A.D., there isn't certainty regarding its origins. In ancient literature, Palamêde, companion of Ulysses, invented chess to amuse his fellow soldiers during the siege of Troy. In one legend, chess was invented in China by General Han Xin during the Han Dynasty in the second century B.C. where it was supposedly developed from the game *Xiangqi* in order to occupy soldiers and prevent debauchery and drunkenness during a siege. Another possible precursor to chess referred to as *Siang-Ki* was documented in writings more than 2000 years ago. The game gained popularity in Japan as the game of *go* which began with an empty board and pieces of the same value. Instead of limiting an opponent's pieces' movements, the goal of the game was to control the most territory.

Historians identify Northwest India around 600 A.D. as a possible site and time of origin for chess. In one story, the Queen of Ceylon invented chess to distract her husband from his worries. In another story—here the game was called *chaturanga*—a Brahmin named Sissa wanted to teach the tyrant Rajah Balhait that a ruler cannot function without his subjects. In recompense for winning at *chaturanga*, Sissa requested that he be given one measure of wheat for the first win, two for the second, four for the third, and eight for the fourth, the measures of wheat doubling with each win. The Rajah accepted this idea but had not calculated that the game would end with Sissa owning more wheat than was stored in the entire nation.

The early form of chess in the sixth century called *chaturanga*, however, is not the earliest, as there are images of chess that date much further back, for example, a wall painting in the tomb of Queen Nefertiti of Egypt dating from 1250 B.C., exists in which the queen is playing with what resemble chess pieces. Excavations of a shipwreck near Serce Limani, (opposite Rhodes, off the coast of Turkey) brought to light eight wooden chess pieces from circa 1025, suggesting that the game was known in the Mediterranean region by the late tenth to early eleventh centuries. The National Museum in Copenhagen has an chess piece of an enthroned figure (shown here) made of ivory.

In the sixth century A.D., the Sassanians in Persia were also said to play chess. Chess was a royal and intellectual game in Persia. The oldest chess books are Arabic and date to approximately 850 A.D. In the mid-ninth century two manuscripts were written about chess, extracts from the work of Abu Bakr Muhammad bin Yahya al-Suli, among others, and titled *The Book of Chess*. During the reign of Ad-Muktafi, caliph of Baghdad from 902-908 A.D., a chess tournament was staged between the court champion al-Mawardi and al-Suli. Despite the caliph's encouragement of his champion, Al-Suli defeated his opponent. Al-Suli's reputation was unchallenged for over six hundred years and when praising a player, it would be said "he plays like the Maestro al-Suli".

After the Arab conquests, chess spread through Byzantium to Europe in the ninth century A.D. The earliest dateable chess pieces are from seventh-century Samarkand (in modern Uzbekistan), along the Silk Road between the East and West.

In H. J. R. Murray's, *The History of Chess* (1913), the author describes chess simply as a descendant of an Indian game transmitted to the West sometime in the seventh century. Early chess pieces were divided into the four groups of the military: the infantry, cavalry, chariots, and elephants, represented today by the pawn, knight, bishop, and rook. At this point, the game had naturalistic looking chessmen resembling an army in miniature, complete with typically eastern elements, such as elephants and a vizier.[1] Initially chess was a war game with male fighters, on foot or mounted on animals, but due to prohibitions against the portrayal of people and animals, Muslim players used more abstract pieces. The famous Caliph Haren

[1] The only early Indian chess piece extant is in the Cabinet des Medailles, Paris.

● *A Chess Game on a Mirror Case,*
ca. 1300, ivory, 11.5 x 0.90 cm.
Musée du Louvre, Paris

al-Rashid, who reigned from 786-809 A.D. in Baghdad, is credited with popularizing chess, along with backgammon, polo, and archery. The ability to play chess blindfolded could bring admittance to the highest social circles and great riches.

In Persia, the game was called *shatranj* around 600 A.D. and the rules of play were still evolving. The Muslims, after their conquest of Persia, largely retained the game's Persian names when they adopted it. As the game's popularity began to spread, *shatranj* became *ajedres* in Spanish, *xadrez* in Portuguese, and *zatnkion* in Greek.

A set of twelfth-century chess pieces found in Nishapur, Iran (now at the Metropolitan Museum of Art), made of stonepaste, is one of the earliest known. The names of the earliest European pieces are derived from Arabic. Moves in chess mirrored moves in battle, and viewed as an exercise in strategy. In the late tenth century, after winning a chess game against his minister, the Fatimid Caliph Al-Muizz is supposed to have smiled and exclaimed, "How do you expect to rule over Egypt, if you were unable to rule over a chess board?".

At the beginning of the tenth century chess was known in Russia and Scandinavia through trade with the Caliphate of Baghdad. The Vikings introduced chess to Britain and Iceland and circular chess boards have been found in a Norman castle in Gloucester, England,

By the year 1000 chess had probably spread to much of southern Europe due to the course of the Near Eastern conquest of the Iberian penninsula in the eighth century. Simultaneously, it seems to have arrived in Italy from Constantinople. The eleventh century basilica of San Savino in Piacenza has a mosaic pavement section showing a man sitting on an armchair, the hand of his adversary hovering over a chess board. Similar imagery from 1143 is also found in the Palatine chapel in Palermo. According to historians, various theories also suggest that chess spread throughout Europe as a result of the Crusades.

The first written mention we have of chess in France, dates to 1008 and concerns a rock crystal chess set of great value; a game was given by Ermengarde to his sister-in-law made of jet, elephant ivory and crystal. At the monastery of Saint-Gilles du Gard there is another example, willed from Saint of Urgel-Ermengarde I, in which the directional markings on the game were made of a combination of cow, horse, and stag bone inserted into a black background. There is also a cross in the center of the board whose function was perhaps purely ornamental. Precious materials were used for the chess pieces at Saint-Gilles du Gard and Sainte-Foy de Conques. Charlemagne's famous ivory chess pieces have been in the treasury of the Abbey of Saint-Denis, just north of Paris, since the thirteenth-century. The beautifully carved pieces were made in Salerno and date from the end of the eleventh century, establishing a link between southern Italy and the Islamic world of Southern Spain.

Many beautiful antique ivory chess pieces are German. Two examples from Cologne, from about 1100, are in the collection of the Cloisters in New York; one is the blinded Samson led by a boy and another is Hercules slaying Germanium. Ivory was a common material but early chess pieces were also made of materials such as mother of pearl, wood, rock crystal, gold and silver.

Chess pieces made of walrus ivory from Trondheim, Norway (or possibly Iceland) dating between 1150-1200 A.D. were unearthed in 1831 on the Isle of Lewis off the west coast of Scotland, in the Outer Hebrides. The Lewis chess pieces, now at the British Museum and the National Museum of Scotland, include seventy-eight pieces from four incomplete sets which together make up the full cast of characters found on modern boards. These pieces are widely regarded as important indicators of the rising popularity of chess in Europe at the time.

The Lewis pawns are dome-topped octagonal towers over slabs. The king, queen, and bishops (who all have individualized riders) and the knights, riding pony-sized steeds and warders—the old name for the knights—have stupefied expressions and bulging eyes. One of the warders wears a long robe, a conical helmet, carries a shield and sword and wears a quizzical expression. The robes of some warders are slightly rumpled and their teeth overlap the top edge of their shields. The kings sit on thrones carved with interlaced patterns of vines, mystical beasts, and architectural motifs. With slightly stooped shoulders, the kings hold swords on their laps and seem to

● *The Lewis Chess Pieces*, 1150-1200 A.D., ivory and bone. The British Museum, London

---

²   Ottonian Germanus. Gamer, Helena M. *The Earliest Evidence of Chess in Western Literature: The Einsiedein Verses Speculum 29* (October 1954).

be preoccupied. The pieces range in height from 3" to 4" tall (9-10 cm) and were originally divided by color, half were tinted red. The faces, while stylized, are all different, from clean shaven to bearded in various styles.

Einsiedein, a Latin poem by a Benedictine monk, described chess pieces of the late 1200s and the game's detailed rules. The author praised chess by contrast with games of chance because it required neither dice or stakes (religious opposition to gaming and gambling tended to be unequivocal).[2] Even so, some clergy frowned upon chess as a waste of time and a distraction. In the eleventh century, the bishop of Florence was criticized by the reformer Peter Damian, because the bishop made the distinction between chess and dice. As skill was required for chess, this secured the view of chess as a superior game. In poems and literary essays, chess was promoted

as a social accomplishment by the twelfth century.

In Europe, the chessboard reflected Western feudal structures and took on the social dimensions and the social order of the age. The queen replaced the vizier, the horse became a knight, and the chariot was transformed into a tower, today's castle or rook. The elephant became a bishop in France, a jester or a standard bearer in Italy. At this juncture, the queen became an critical piece on the board, second in importance only to the king.[3] Empress Adelaide and her husband Otto I (crowned in 962 as Emperor and Empress of the Holy Roman Empire) and Theophano, wife of Otto II (r. 973-983), were possible inspirations for these chess pieces. The king was always the tallest piece and the queen was usually second in height.[4]

In the Middle Ages in England, chess appears to have been a favorite pastime of the noble class, with tables or backgammon occupying second place. During the Tudor period, the study of chess was considered an essential of a gentleman's education. The medieval chess player placed value on the individual pieces according to the positions

● *King Chesspiece*, German, 14th century. Private collection

● *Spanish Chess Piece*, 12th Century, ivory and bone, 7.1 x 4.4 x 6.8 cm. The Walters Art Museum, Baltimore 71.145

[3] See Alex Hammond, *The Book of Chessmen* (London, 1950) and Janet L. Nelson, "Medieval Queenship", in *Women in Medieval Western European Culture* 193.
[4] See Hans and Siegfried Wichmann, *Chess: The Story of Chess pieces from Antiquity to Modern Times* (New York: Crown, 1964).

each held in society. The knight was thus treated as an equal to the rook, though the rook could move the length of the board and was actually a more powerful piece.

Proficiency at chess became part of the education and culture for people of high rank. The Aragon court physician Moses Cohen, a convert to Christianity in 1106, wrote *Disciplina Clericaus* where he listed the skills necessary "concerning the true nature of nobility", which included riding, swimming, archery, boxing, hawking, verse writing, and chess.[5] The heroes of troubadour poetry were said to be outstanding chess players, as well as fearsome warriors, able hunters, and attentive lovers.[6] Chess and love were also intertwined in Scandinavia. The *Heidarviga Saga* of ca. 1200 tells of a young warrior, Leikner, who courted ladies by "talking or playing chess".[7]

Eleanor of Aquitaine (1122-1204) sought to recreate the court life of Paris with storytellers, troubadours, and games of chance and chess when she made the journey with her first husband, King Louis VII (r.1131-1180), to the Holy Land during the Second Crusade in 1147. Arriving at Constantinople, Eleanor and the king found "twenty thousand knights dressed in silk and white ermine with great marten skins reaching down to their feet, playing chess and backgammon".[8]

When Eleanor's supported her son in a revolt against his father—her second husband, Henry II of England (r. 1154-1189)—she was imprisoned for more than nine years, during which time she was, however, granted a chess partner.[9] Such a precedent had been set earlier when Robert, Duke of Normandy (ca. 1000-1035), who had lost England to his younger brother, Henry I (r. 1100-1135) was permitted a chess partner during his lifetime imprisonment. King Jean II (the Good) of France (r. 1350-1364) was able to purchase an expensive chess set while waiting to be ransomed during a four-year imprisonment.

The Knights Templar were prohibited any game played for stakes. In a description by the Abbot of Clairvaux in 1135 mentions that when "resting from their warfare against the infidels, a thing which rarely occurs, they avoid games of chess and tables".

The queen figure in chess first appeared in Europe at the end of the twelfth century, inspired by the powerful

[5] Victor Keats, *Chess in Jewish History and Hebrew Literature* (Jerusalem: Jerusalem Magnes Press, 1995), p. 59.
[6] *Ibid.*, p. 59.
[7] H.J.R. Murray, *History of Chess* (1913), p. 739.
[8] Aucassin and Nicolette, Glyn S. Burgess, and Elizabeth Anne Cobby, *The Pilgrimage of Charlemagne* (New York & London: Garland Press, 1988.)
[9] See Charles K. Wilkinson and Jessie McNab Dennis, *Chess, East & West, Past & Present* (New York: Metropolitan Museum of Art, 1968).

queens of the period. The previously abstract form in the Arabic chess game resembled the knight (or foot solider), a suggestion for the piece's function. The great variety of chess pieces sculpted in the Middle Ages points to the large zone of diffusion in the Western world. A chess piece of a queen on a throne, probably Spanish, now in the Walters Art Museum in Baltimore, and dating from the twelfth century is shown here.

The Holy Roman Emperor Emperor Frederick II Hohenstaufen (r. 1220-1250) was a patron of science and the arts, a great linguist, wrote a treatise on falconry, and was also an outstanding chess player. His example inspired Italian players, especially those from Lombardy, who became famous chess players throughout Europe. Prior to this Spain had produced the finest players in Europe.

In 1250 the leader of the sect called the Assassins, wished to cease paying tribute to the Templars and the Hospitalers, so he sent an emissary to King Louis IX of France (r. 1226-1270) with a peace proposal. The accompanying gifts were the mark of highest friendship and included the Assassin's own shirt and gold ring, draughts (checkers) and chessboards adorned with amber, as well as a live elephant and a crystal giraffe. King Louis sent the Ishmaelite chief, in return, "scarlet robes, gold cups, and silver vases, not to be outdone!".[10]

The famous manuscript commissioned in 1283 by King Alfonso X of Leon and Castile, *Chess, Dice and Boards* (*Libro de los juegos*) had one hundred and fifty beautiful illustrations and of these sixty chess miniatures. In twenty of these, women players appear (the game was considered a fitting pastime for ladies), in the images queens teach the game to their children, and a nun teaches a novitiate. In some illustrations Moors play against female Christians, and even the king is shown playing opposite a Moorish woman. King Edward I of England (r. 1272-1307), a devoted chess player, is shown playing chess with his future wife, Eleanor of Castile (Alfonso X's half-sister). Edward I and Eleanor of Castile were both avid chess players, and Edward certainly played for money. Eleanor's jasper and crystal chessmen were inherited by her sister-in-law, Isabella of France. Eleanor's borrowed the chess manual of Alfonso X and became competent enough to manage

[10] Thomas Kneightley, *Secret Societies of the Middle Ages* (London, 1837), p. 279.

"Four Kings", the four-player version of the game. King Edward's second wife Maguerite of France, whom he married in 1299, and their children Thomas and Edmund, played chess and tables (backgammon).

A book called *Bonus Socius,* written in abridged Latin in late thirteenth-century Italy (now at the *Biblioteca Nazionale* in Florence) contained over one hundred chess problems with illustrations. *The Book of the Customs of Men and the Duties of Nobles,* or *The Book of Chess,* was based on sermons delivered between 1275 and 1300 by Jacobus de Cessollis, a Dominican friar from Lombardy. The book sold extensively and was translated into at least seven languages. De Cessollis compared the pursuit of chess with the goals of life; this and later works of the type were called "moralities". Many such texts on chess published in this period were devoted to allegorical and symbolic interpretations of the chess game.

Arabshah, the Syrian biographer of Timur (Tamerlane) wrote that Timur thought that, "the game of chess . . . might sharpen his intellect, but his mind was too lofty to play at the lesser game of chess and therefore he played only the greater game, in which the chessboard comprised additional squares, having been increased by two camels, two giraffes, two sentinels, two mantelets (war engines), a vizier, and other pieces". To this day, the most demanding game is known as "Tamerlane chess".

Literary sources mention that chess was played on pieces of embroidered silk or linen fabrics as well as boards placed on the floor. The Museum of Qatar has a fourteenth to fifteenth century silk on cotton-foundation carpet, probably from Samarkand, depicting a flower-strewn field with a chessboard incorporated in its design.

In fourteenth century France, chess was the prestigious accessory of a luxurious home. Guillaume de Metz described the house that Jacques Duchie built as having "[a] room . . . filled with pictures and coats of arms, another with musical instruments, a third was filled with chess games". Among the fabulous treasures of Jean, Duc de Berry (1340-1416) were gaming tables and jeweled chessboards of jasper and rock crystal.[11] The duke owned miniscule ivory spheres within which carved figures played chess. Marguerita of Austria owned fifteenth century chess

[11] See Jules Guiffrey, *Inventory of Jean, Duc de Berry vol. II* (1894-1896).

pieces of sculpted gold and silver with a matching board. One fifteenth-century chess board of Burgundian manufacture, now at the Bargello Museum of Florence, has borders of ivory decorated with gallant scenes.

In 1456 William Caxton published a book on chess with his own printing press that ranked immediately after the Bible in sales. By 1475, changes to the game of chess saw the evolution of chess into its modern form as chess had become *the* popular game. Italy and Spain adopted the basic moves and printed books on chess such as *Repetition de Amores y arte de Ajedres (Training in the Love and Art of Chess)* by Luis Ramirez de Lucena, published in Salamanca in 1497, and Ruy Lopes de Segura's *Libro de la Invencion liberal y arte del juego des Axedres* (Book of the Liberal Invention of Art of Playing Chess) in 1561.

King Henry VIII (r. 1509-1547) of England owned several costly *bourdes* for the *wittie plai of the cheastes*. Louis XIII of France (r. 1610-1643) was a precocious and fine chess player and so were many of the courtiers who adopted his interest. Game boards, such as the one illustrated here, were compact and portable. They figure frequently in still life and *vanitas* pictures, such as Lubin Baugin's *Still-life with Chessboard* (The Five Senses) of 1630, now in the Musée du Louvre.

Highly refined and expensive game boards made with *pique d'or*, tortoise shell, ivory, rock crystal, lacquer, and elaborate inlay work were produced for rulers, the nobility, wealthy bankers and merchants in Italy, France, and Northern Europe. Such chessboards were important gifts, bequeathed to church treasuries by nobles. As early as the beginning of the eleventh century, Count Ermengarde of Urgel (Catalonia) left his valuable chessmen to the French convent of Saint Giles, "for the work of the church".[12]

The king's moves in the game seem to have been formulated during the first half of the seventeenth century. By this point, the game was won by the capture of the adversary's king in a checkmate. The queen, who had her first appearance in twelfth-century Spain, had undergone changes in power, gender, and name. Initially she was allowed to move only one square diagonally, making her one of the weakest pieces on the board. Only in the fifteenth century did she attain her present position of power. One story has it that Caterina Sforza was the model for the warrior queen. Caterina Sforza was married to a weak prince who did not rule his territory so she donned armor and led her troops into battle, protecting her husband, and collecting taxes. Since then the Queen has been the most powerful piece on the board.

Differences in the iconography of chess existed in Protestant and Catholic countries. In Catholic lands, the chess queen was a symbol of the Holy Mother. The name *reine* in French and *dame* were attached to the Virgin, as Queen of Heaven and *Nôtre Dame*. By contrast, at the end of the fifteenth century, Protestants used the word *königin* or "queen" as the name of the second tallest figure, forgoing any religious connotations.

In Germany, chess, backgammon, and a game called *glückshaus*, could be combined in one game board box. An example, intricately inlaid with tulips, other flowers and foliate designs in olivewood, walnut, ebony, rosewood, and boxwood, can be seen pictured here.

The Archduchess Margaret of Austria (1480-1530)—who reared her nephew, the future Emperor Charles V—was a great collector and poet (she also "painted skillfully"), and probably had the finest library outside of Italy, which included many books on chess.

[12]   Murray, *Ibid.*, p. 406.

Pope Leo X (1475-1521) known as the "pontiff of the golden age" and praised by artists and men of letters, including Erasmus, was known for his magnanimity, learning, love of peace, kindness and humanity. He spent his leisure time playing chess and cards. He almost bankrupted the Vatican with his expenditures for the amusement of the court and the people of Rome.

Catherine de' Medici (1519-1589) was also reputed to be a fine player of chess. Queen of France and mother of three sixteenth-century French kings, she had cupboards filled with games lining the walls in her private palace, including chess boards and miniature billiards. Moreover, included among her approximately 4,500 books and 750 manuscripts were manuals on chess playing. She did not have the opportunity, but her great wish was to challenge Paolo Boi of Syracuse, the celebrated Italian chess champion. There were already famous chess players in the sixteenth and seventeenth centuries, such as the Spaniard Ruy Lopez and the Italians Polerio and Gioacchino Greco, called "the Calabrese". Innocenzo Ringhieri's 1557 book *Cento giuochi liberali et d'ingegno* (One Hundred Games of Ingenuity), games for female players, was dedicated to Catherine de' Medici.

Chess was considered a royal game. Many courts in Northern Italy had a court master who taught young nobles. Commoners were initially banned from playing chess, and punished if caught playing the game, but chess nonetheless spread to the general population. In Italy the customers of Milanese barbershops were not allowed to play games involving gambling, only to play draughts or chess.

In 1656, a Venetian reported that the ambassador from Moscow and his staff did not go to Mass on holidays and instead stayed home to play chess, a game which they were said to play masterfully. A French chronicle of 1685 comparing the French to chess-playing foreign diplomats at the court of Louis XIV admitted, "our best players are school children compared to them".[13] A book published in 1696 entitled *Divertissemens innocens, contenant les Regles du jeu des échecs, du billard, de la paume, du palle-mail, et du tric trac* (Innocent Entertainments: with the Rules of Chess, Billiards, de la Paume, Palle-Mail and Tric-Trac) in the Hague by Adrian Moetjens, had sections on billiards, *la*

[13] Marilyn Yolom, *Birth of a Chess Queen* (New York: Harper Collins, 2004), p. 174.

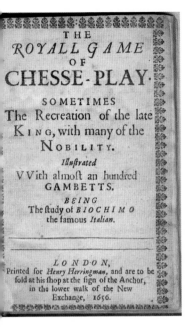

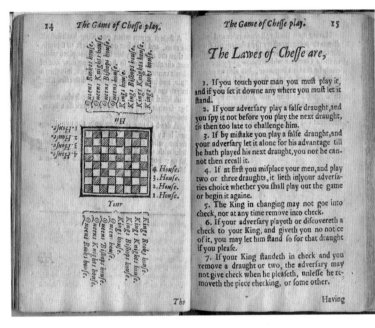

Gioachino Greco, *Chess Manual*, ca. 1646. Private Collection

paume, palle-mail, and backgammon. The text has more than three hundred pages on chess with discussions of different openings and situations. Also included were engravings depicting daily activities.

A member of an old Parisian bourgeois family, Sire M. Baillet, who had a passion for gambling and music, had a music room—he played the harp, organ, hurdy-gurdy, guitar, and psalteries—and also a game room filled with all manner of games and chessboards, prefiguring the fashion for gaming and music rooms in the eighteenth century.

France became the center of chess activity in the eighteenth century, led by the musician and composer of *opera comique*, François-André Danican Philidor (1726-1795). A great player—the "Philidor defense" is a famous defensive strategy—he was trained by M. de Kermar, Sire de Légal, himself a leading light of the *Café de la Régence* (the Parisian center for chess players until the early twentieth century). Philidor wrote a book on chess in 1749, *Analyse du jeu des échêcs* (*An Analysis of Chess*) which went through more editions and translations than any other book on the game.

Fifteen years after Philador's death, Howard Staunton played at Simpson's Divan (the English equivalent of the

Café de la Régence) championing the "Staunton pattern" of standardized chess pieces. Staunton defeated the French champion St-Amant in 1843 and was one of the earliest players to use what is known as the Franchetti method. Staunton called himself "world champion" and organized the first international tournament, but was beaten in the semi-finals by the German Adolf Anderssen in 1851. Anderssen went on to win important chess games, the "Immortal Game" and the "Evergreen" played in 1851 and 1852, respectively; the former in which he sacrificed his queen and rook to win.

During Napoleon's exile on the island of Saint Helena, he played chess frequently. He had often played during pauses in battle, and though he was considered a great military strategist, he was not a particularly able chess player. He hated being beaten! Napoleon had hoped to leave his son at the helm of the Western world, with Rome as its crown jewel, and instead he left him a fine game of *hombre* that he had played in exile; it was eventually donated to the Napoleonic Museum in Rome.

Russia has a very rich chess history. During the reign of Empress Catherine the Great, chess was the most popular game in Russia.[14] One English visitor noted:

Chess is so common in Moscow; I scarcely enter into any company where parties were not engaged in that diversion and I very frequently observed in my passage

[14] Noted by Richard Twiss in *Chess* (1787).

through the streets, the tradesmen and common people playing it before the doors of their shops or houses. The Russians are esteemed greatly proficient in chess.[15]

Russian priests had been exhorted not to read forbidden books, use charms or magic, watch horse races, play chess or dice. In the fifteenth century a clergyman could be dismissed for engaging in the game. In ecclesiastic rules, keeping hawks, beasts, birds, or playing chess could be the cause of expulsion from an order. Orthodox Russians were discouraged from playing chess until the eighteenth century when the church gave up and chess became Russia's most popular pastime.[16]

Today there are many more elite chess players than ever before. The "Game of the Century" in 1956 made Bobby Fischer a champion at age thirteen (a game he won by also sacrificing his queen), he became a grand master at fifteen years and six months! The Hungarian Judit Polgar became a grandmaster at age fifteen years and four months in 1991. The record is now held by Sergey Karjakin of Russia, grand master at only twelve.

Kirsan Ilyumzhinov, the president of FIDE (*Fédération Internationale des Échecs*) and national chess champion (at the age of fourteen) of Kalmnyk, an autonomous republic of the U.S.S.R., became, at forty-four, President of Kalmnyk. Upon his election in 1993, he abolished parliament, made changes to the constitution and lengthened the term of his office. A state directive supported the development of a chess; study of chess was required of every student in the first through third grades. Seventeen Kalmnyk students have ranked in FIDE in the past ten years—a remarkable feat given the state has only 300,000 residents. He built a "chess city" at the cost of fifty million dollars for the 1998 chess Olympiad and planned to have "rapid chess" replace the "silent hours" where players mull over their next move.[17]

Many children in New York City and other parts of the United States have chess groups, with competition starting from as early as four years of age. Chess computers are now used for extensive training. At Intermediate School 318 in Williamsburg, Brooklyn, the average age of players on the chess team is just under thirteen. Students (coming from a demographic with more than a 70% poverty rate)

[15] Quoted in John T. Alexander, *Catherine the Great: Life & Legend* (Oxford: Oxford University Press, 1989).

[16] More recently, chess was banned in Iran from 1979 to 1988 (along with other activities such as watching television, playing billiards and kite-flying).

[17] Michael Specter, "Planet Kirsan", in *The New Yorker* (April 24, 2006), pp. 112-122

have won seven national championships. They consistently defeat teams from the top private schools, doing class homework during their lunch breaks and assigning the rest of their time to chess.[18]

The Harlem chess matches played in St. Nicolas Park near 141st Street in New York City draw crowds and create street chess legends. In winter, the matches moves indoors to a chess and backgammon club on 139th Street. The regulars include a variety of players, from Wall Street brokers to chess and backgammon hustlers.

Jacqueline Piatigorsky, a member of the Rothschild family, and her husband, the cellist Gregor Piatigorsky, together sponsored many historic chess matches. For one competition, the Soviets allowed their world champions Tigran Petrosian (from Soviet Armenia) and Paul Keres (from Estonia) to travel abroad to play; they tied for first place, followed by Bobby Fischer. In 1966, one hundred and ten players competed in the Piatigorsky cup with Boris Spassky coming in first. This match was at the height of the Cold War and called the "Cold War Battle". It was broadcast in sport fashion and was watched by a huge audience. The world became chess mad and millions of chess sets were sold. In addition to being a sponsor, Mrs. Piatigorsky was the 2nd ranking female international player in 1953, and won a bronze medal playing for the USA in the Netherlands.

Chess is still so popular that when Judit Polgar made a brilliant counter-attack during the Elista Competition, the game was reported in its entirety in a New York newspaper. Another recent article spoke of the victory of Alexander Grischuk (a very skilled player despite the fact that he divides his time between chess and poker) over Sergei Rublevsky. Chess grandmaster Maurice Ashley was recently pictured in a New York newspaper playing thirty simultaneous opponents in New York's Central Park as part of a monthly series on chess personalities.

Roger Caillois (1913-1978) analyzed the game of poker as having four components: luck, competition, calculation, and risk/excitement, in which he found luck and calculation equal. In chess, however, luck hardly enters into the game.

Competitive chess at the highest levels can be lucrative.

[18]   Elizabeth Green Weiss, *New York Sun* (May 21, 2007).

Liberale da Verona,
The Chess Players, ca. 1475.
The Metropolitan Museum of
Art, New York

The **FIDE** 2013 Chess World Championship held in Chennai India, has an approximately $2.5 million prize. The competition between Viswanathan Anand of India and Magnus Carlsen of Norway resulted in a win for Carlsen, who was 22.

Benjamin Franklin wrote, "The game of chess is not merely an idle amusement, several very valuable qualities of the mind, useful in the course of human life, are to be acquired and strengthened by it so as to become ready on all occasions; for life is a kind of chess in which we have often points to gain, and competitors or adversaries to contend with, in which there is a vast variety of good and ill events that are, in some degree, the effect of prudence or want of it".[19]

[19] Benjamin Franklin *The Morals of Chess* (1779).

Figures Playing Checkers,
German, 18th Century.
Private Collection

Checkers

No gamer was ever yet a happy man.
William Corbett, *Advice to Young Men*, 1829

Checkers, although it is a simpler game, is related to chess. It is called *gioco della dama* or *cronometrista* in Italian, and like chess, is of ancient origin. A game similar to checkers is known to have been played by Egyptian pharaohs around 1600 B.C. Homer and Plato make references to a game that resembles checkers. The Arc and Historical Museum in Bukhara (Central Asia) has on display checkers from the tenth century made of black ebony. The pieces are variously formed with indented segments like little domed hats.

Checkers (also known as draughts) possibly originated in the South of France around 1000 A.D. as a game called *fierges* or *fers*, meaning "queen" in a dialect of medieval French. The *Chronicle* of Philip Mouskat, written in 1243, mentions a "King of *Ferges*". As in checkers, a *fer* could be promoted to a king. Later, the *dame* became the *jeu de dames* or checkers. The capture of a piece at risk became obligatory, and if the opportunity was missed, the penalty, known as *jeu forcé*, was the removal of the piece from the board.

A treatise on checkers was published in 1547 by the Spaniard, Antonio de Torquemada, and by then the modern version had evolved. The fashionable young men mentioned in Giovanni Boccaccio's *Decameron* of 1353 played both checkers and chess. In addition to backgammon and chess, checkers was also a popular pastime for knights in early sixteenth-century Europe. An early eighteenth-century checkerboard (shown here) is unusual for having survived in such fine condition. It was made with precious materials of red lacquer, tortoise, and *pique d'or*.

● Milton Bradley, *The Checkered Game of Life*, 1866

The *Journal des Garde Meubles* in eighteenth century Paris mentions numerous game tables delivered to the court where checkers, called *dames* or *echequier* in French, was much enjoyed. The checkerboard with one hundred squares substituted the former one, which had sixty-four.

Louis-Léopold Boilly, *Game of Billiards*, 1807, oil on canvas. The State Hermitage Museum, St. Petersburg

Billiards

To play billiards well is the sign of a misspent youth
Herbert Spencer (quoting an unknown source), ca. 1680

In Shakespeare's *Antony and Cleopatra*, Cleopatra invites her attendant to play billiards, not the only mention of games in Shakespeare; elsewhere Miranda and Ferdinand play chess soon after their wedding in *The Tempest*. In *The Travels of Anacharisis*, the early-sixth century Scythian philosopher is the subject of an imaginary travel journal—from the northern shores of the Black Sea to Athens—published by the French Jesuit scholar Jean Jacques Barthelemy (1716-1795). Described therein is a game analogous to our billiards!

As early as the second century A.D., an Irish king, Catkire More, is said to have had fifty-five brass billiard balls, pool tables, and cues in his estate. France, Italy, Spain, and Germany have all been considered the country of origin for the game of billiards as it is known today. The name is derived from the French word *bille*, meaning stick. In the 1674 *The Compleat Gamester* by Charles Cotton, the author understood billiards to have been played first in Italy and then Spain. Billiards was also associated with bowls (*boccia* in Italian), which may have been the origin of this version.

The first billiard table we know about was built in Elbeuf, Normandy, in 1429, and was a slab of stone covered with a fabric drapery. French billiard tables quickly developed into the tables we recognize today with four legs, four cushions on the inside-rim, and a base for play covered with green baize or felt. Initially there were no holes or pockets built into the table. In an eighteenth-century drawing by Pietro Novelli, shown here, Venetians play billiards in a tavern on a billiards table that is recognizably modern.

Giuseppe Zocchi, *I billiardi*, 1750. Museo dell'Opificio di Pietre Dure, Florence

Billiards was first played in France at the time of Louis XI (r. 1461-1483) as an easier version of the ancient game of *paille-maille* (*le jeu du maille*, pall mall or *pelle melle*). The lawn game was the forerunner of croquet and golf and played by people of wealth. *Paille-maille* required leaning down and bending, and therefore required more (or too much) effort! Billiards was recommended to Louis XIV by his physician as suitable exercise and the king played often at Versailles.

Billiards was played at the court of Louis XVI where Marie Antoinette was an avid participant, even the *Petit Hameau* at Versailles was equipped with a billiard room She would make her appearance at eleven o'clock at night to take up a game, an activity described by an English army officer at the French court in December, 1784:

> After dinner the Duke of Dorset [the English ambassador] asked me and Mr. Coxe to go with him [to] the Duchesse of Polignac where we saw the Queen who made an apology for not receiving the presentations. (She had not been out of her chamber since her lying-in). After-

wards her majesty sat down to *tric-trac*, and afterwards went to billiards. Her majesty asked me if I could play. I answered no. She plays very well.[1]

Another reference to the queen's royal pastime is made by Madame Duchesse de Tourzel: "after dining she played a game of billiards with the king so that he would get a little exercise. She was too depressed to go to the spectacle of the court while Paris was in ferment". The value Marie Antoinette placed on her particularly fine billiard cue is recounted by Madame Campan:

● Pietro Antonio Novelli, *The Interior of an Inn with Figures Seated at a Table*, 18th Century, black chalk, pen and brown ink, brown wash, additional red chalk, 382 x 330 mm

● Giovanni Grevembroch, Nobles Playing Billiards from *Venetian Dress,* 18th Century. Biblioteca Museo Correr, Venice

An evening when the Queen returned from the Duchesse's (de Vaudreuil), she asked her *valet de chambre* to bring the billiard cue that was in her cabinet and ordered me to open the case that contained it. I was

[1] John Lough, *British Travelers Observations* (1763-1788).

astonished not to find the padlock where she kept the key on her watch chain. I opened the case and pulled out the cue in two pieces. It was of ivory and had been made of one elephant tusk. The *crosse* was of gold worked with infinite taste. "Look", Marie Antoinette said then, "in what manner M. de Vaudreuil 'arranged' a jewel to which I attached great value. I left it on the *canapé* while I was speaking to the duchesse in the salon. He used it, and with an angry movement for a blocked ball, he hit the cue so violently against the billiard table that it broke in two. The noise made me enter the room; I didn't say a word but looked at him with the air of malcontent that penetrated me".[2]

Madame Guérnénee, one of the Queen's ladies, was addicted to billiards and her gambling debts created a scandal. Her husband, too, went bankrupt, to the tune of thirty-two million *écus*. As a result, their property at Montreuil was put up for sale and purchased by Louis XVI who pre-

● Giuseppe Bernardino Bison, *The Billiard Players, Caffe degli Specchi, Trieste*, late 18th Century-early 19th Century, gouache

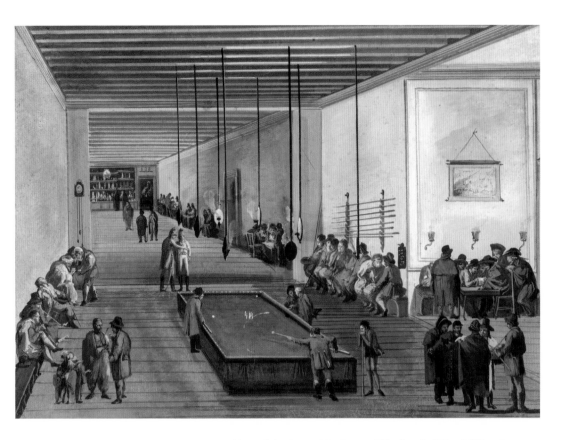

Giuseppe Bernardino Bison, *The Billiard Players, Caffe degli Specchi, Trieste*, late 18th Century-early 19th Century, gouache

sented it to his sister Madame Elisabeth. The billiard room in the house had light from seven *croisées* (chandeliers) looking out to the *cour d'honneur* (courtyard).

Louis XVI played billiards with his sister the night before he gave himself up to the Assembly as the French Revolution began in earnest on August 9, 1792. In fact, the game of *trou-madame*, published in an almanac in 1791, was called "an ancient game, very well known, and the cause of all the Revolutions".[3] After Louis XVI, Napoleon, too, was known to play billiards.

During the reign of Charles X of France (r. 1824-1830), the artist Henrique Devigne laid down the rules and forms for the game of billiards as we now know them. The game of pool is derived from billiards, though it has different regulations, and billiards itself has several versions of play.

The billiards table underwent stylistic changes, as with the furnishings of the period. The cathedral style table designed by Percier and Fontaine for Napoleon and also

2   *Mémoires de Madame Campan (Premiere femme de chambre de Marie Antoinette)*. Mercure de France, pp. 232-233.
3   *Almanach du Trou-Madame* (1791).

made in Louis Philippe's time (r. 1830-1848) were made of somber woods such as mahogany. Under Napoleon III there was a shift to lighter colored wood with inlays. In the second half of the eighteenth century, lighter woods were already used in England for billiards tables.

In France, Madame de Cayla ordered a billiard table in the neo-gothic style for her ch,teau at Saint-Ouen which was displayed in the Exhibition of Industrial Products in 1827. The nineteenth century saw an explosion of billiard tables as they became fashionable for the well-to-do. Many billiards tables had marquetry with mythological subjects and a pastiche of everything from *chinoiserie* to military designs.

Billiard tables have survived due to their solidity, although mostly later nineteenth century models are seen at auction. The example shown here was made sometime during the period of Charles X and Louis Philippe.

Having a billiard room became a requisite of wealthy society in New York. George and Emma Bellows formed a billiards club with artists and friends, including Robert Henri and John Sloan, at the National Arts Club at Gramercy Park in Manhattan.

● *Tuebingen Students Playing Tree-ball Pocket Billiards*, early 19th Century

Vincent Van Gogh, *The Night
Cafe*, 19th Century, Yale Art
Gallery, New Haven,
Connecticut

Il Nobilissimo gioco del Ingerio from
Venice, 18th Century. Private Collection

Roulette

*No one can win at roulette unless he steals money
from the table when the croupier isn't looking.*
Albert Einstein

Roulette is probably of French origin—some sources
state that the game was first played in Paris—and may
have been invented by Blaise Pascal (1623-1662) during a
monastic retreat. Other sources says its origin is Chinese;
thirty-seven animal statuettes were arranged into a "magic
square", and play resembled that of roulette. In still other
accounts, roulette was played in Tibet and transported west
by French Dominican friars, one of whom replaced the stat-
uettes with numbers from zero to thirty-six.

Roulette, as we know it, was most probably first played
in Paris at the end of the eighteenth century. It was preced-
ed by an English game called Even and Odd, popular in the
early eighteenth century. This game had a wheel and its in-
novation was the throwing of a little ball onto the circular
turning deck to see if the number came out odd or
even. The Museum of the Lotterie Nationale has an exam-
ple of this game.

Biribissi (also called *cavagnole*) required a decorated
board for play, was a game of chance like a lottery and an
early version of roulette. By the late eighteenth century,
roulette had already become fashionable in European casi-
nos where the roulette wheel was of slightly convex shape
and had separations. In simpler circles the players used
dried beans or orange peel to cover the numbers, rather
than counters. Being the first to cover the numbers or get-
ting through a series of moves before anyone else was one
way of playing, not unlike today's bingo.

The Venetian game *Il Nobilissimo gioco del Ingerio* (an eigh-
teenth century example is shown here) has, like a modern
roulette wheel, an iron compass that can be spun. The ar-
rows point to a variety of objects painted on the outer cir-

cle including a bear, a wolf, a goat, a dog, a wet nurse, a clock-keeper, a whale, a cello, a hunter, a pirate, an astrologer, a farmer, a fortress, a compass, and a bed. The name of the object was written on the inner circle below the image. A similar wheel, labeled *Nobilissimo Gioco della Mea,* in the collection of the Museo Correr in Venice is beautifully decorated with *arte povera* (painted and lacquered engravings). A similar game, *Il Nobile giuoco della cavagnola,* was also popular in Venice.

🔵 *Caricature of Gambling at an Early Roulette Table,* ca. 1800

The Russian author and playright Anton Chekhov (1860-1904) described roulette in a 1891 letter written on his first to trip to Europe. He wrote of "a little place called Monte Carlo, where roulette is played" and described it thus:

> The Monte Carlo halls have big roulette tables . . . I went there on my third day here, and lost. Gambling is horribly seductive. After we'd lost our money, I sat down with Suvorin's son and we thought long and hard about working out an infallible system of winning. We went back yesterday with 500 francs each, my first stake was two gold sovereigns, then I won again and again, the pockets of my waistcoat were weighed down with gold, as well as Belgian, Italian, Greek and Austrian money . . . I've never seen so

much gold and silver. I started to play at five o'clock, and by ten o'clock hadn't a franc left; all I had was the comforting thought that at least I had my return ticket to Nice. Of course you will say, "what a dreadful things to do, here we are starving, while he plays roulette!". You are quite right, and have my full permission to slit my throat. But I am pleased with myself: at least I shall now be able to tell my grandchildren that I have played roulette and have some experience of the feelings the game stimulates.[1]

When roulette is played in a European casino the house percentage on "odds" or "even" is 1 13/27%, and, as all other types of wagers, the bank grosses 2 26/37%. By contrast, in America the house has the advantage of a "0" and a double "0" (unlike the single "0" in Europe) so the bank gains 5 5/19% of all bets (except for line or 5 number bets) and the house's percentage is 7 7/19%. Roulette is a better gamble in Europe!

[1]   Anton Chekhov, *A Life in Letters* (London: Penguin Books, 2004), p. 276.

Venetian Red Lacquer Flipper Game, mid-18th Century, Museé de la Lotterie, Brussels, Belgium

Games and Gambling:
Present and Future

The better the gambler, the worse the man.
Pubilius Syrus, Rome, ca. 41 B.C.

The State of Games and Game Playing Today

Chess is still a popular game around the world. The United States Chess Federation has 47,000 members; 290 are masters and thirteen members are under the age of fourteen. Union Square and Washington Square Park in Manhattan are still centers where players can test their skill against the regulars, while in Harlem; chess has been concentrated at St. Nicolas Park and 141th Street for decades. In 2013 a play was performed at the New York City Park Avenue Armory called *The Machine,* which focused on the pivotal 1997 chess match between Gary Kasparov and the IBM computer Deep Blue. Chess is still a game that continues to fascinate.

Backgammon, though a specialist game, is still being played worldwide. A Norwegian computer science student at the University of Oslo named Fredrik Dahl has worked on artificial intelligence for government projects specializing in two-sided zero-sum games. Dahl, a keen backgammon player, has used computers to improve his game. He created a program to predict the probability for winning backgammon from every position on the board and at every stage, and to have the program discover strategies by itself. Dahl then turned to programming for poker. Dahl's machine had to be taught a perfect defensive game and be hard to beat. By 2006, billions of hands had been played on the computer from which the program 'learned' random, unpredictable moves, including an optimal number of bluffs.

Harrah's, operator of the World Series of Poker, which operates on the Isle of Man in the Irish Sea, estimates revenue of $1 billion annually. In Brooklyn, a federal district court threw out the conviction in 2012 of the man who ran a warehouse on Staten Island where poker games took place. The one hundred and twenty page ruling said that poker is more a game of skill than chance and therefore should not be prosecuted under federal law, which otherwise prohibits running an illegal gambling business. It is not yet clear whether the US attorney's office will appeal the case.

People will play at casinos and slot machines knowing the odds are against them. The casinos at Las Vegas have slot machines with themes ranging from "Spider Man" to deep-sea fishing. The slot machines were first introduced in 1895, and have seen incredible advances since then; casino operators can rapidly alter payouts, raise or reduce betting or minimums, and change the games for a specific audience. One machine, *Texas Hold'Em Poker*, plays the limited version of the popular game so well that the machines can beat very skilled poker players. While a player can win with sheer luck, the machines are bound to win because they have been programmed to play aggressively and unpredictably with expertise provided by champion professionals. Poker is a game of intuition and skill, bluffs and traps and the new machine plays with optimal strategies.

Gregg Giuffria, whose company makes gambling machines, sold a patent (released by the Defense Department to the public sector) to The International Gaming Technology Co. Giuffria decided to develop card-playing software into a casino machine. He had poker professionals play against the machine, which they couldn't beat. Digitized cards, chips, and sound effects were incorporated into the machine with the traditional green felt depicted on the screen. Since the machine was unbeatable, they had to reduce the machines' infallibility, so it didn't beat humans all the time. There are now 200 machines in the typical casino and just as many people, if not more trying to figure out how to beat them!

Traditional board games have migrated to computers, the internet and, increasingly, to smart phones. With applications specially designed for these formats, players can access games on their cell phones and through social media and can "virtually" play with others. *Monopoly Live*,

Slot machine, USA, ca. 1950

which costs about fifty dollars, issues instruction through a speaker. It keeps track of money and sees that players adhere to the rules. Its manufacturer, Hasbro, believes that young players do not want to read instructions and would prefer to have instructions issued by spoken word (though most adults don't like to read instructions either). Millions of people now play *Scrabble* on tiny screens, wherever they are, against players anywhere in the world. A similar game called *Words with Friends*, created by Zynga, has 292 million monthly active users. These games try to combat monotony by introducing random events emphasizing social interaction. Being able to negotiate with others, make up one's own rules, and argue with other players makes a successful video or on-line game.[1]

The on-line game *Magic*, pits two players in strategic combat, with cards representing spells, magical lands and creatures. Players collect and trade cards to personalize their decks. Scholarships have been awarded to *Magic* players for college through a non-profit organization which assists students who play this fantasy trading card game. *Magic* has weekly events, with international purses that can reach two hundred and fifty thousand dollars.

The American Council on Science and Public Health has stated that video games are addictive. Indeed, the American Medical Association is considering classifying video game addiction in the same category as compulsive gambling or dependence on drugs and alcohol. A food product company has garnered information that 71% of young men in the USA play video games for more than six hours per week. Video games were found to be more relevant to young men than sports, music or films, according to company findings. *Game Stop*, the video game retailer already has more than 4,300 locations and there are over 50,000 mobile games on the market in the USA. Headsets exist which include a mixer that allow video game players to blend their games with chat and phone calls.

There are physical ramifications to all the video game playing; as recently reported by Dr. Mohamed Khan, as many as 15% of players who indulge for more than two hours a day experience setbacks such as seizures and ten-

[1]   Joey Lee, an Assistant Professor of Technology and Education at Teachers College, Columbia University.

donitis. On the other hand, a new school sponsored by the Game Lab Institute of Play, will explore "new ways of thinking, acting, and speaking through playing" and The John D. and Catherine T. MacArthur Foundation donated $1.2 million for its planning and development. Researchers in a study funded over the past four years by the University of California at San Francisco on video game playing and the older brain, have discovered that octogenarians show improved short-term memory and the same long-term focus, as people in their twenties after playing video games for a certain amount of time.

Game producers are now offering ways for players to improve their cognitive skills, their memory, and help them solve difficult problems with video games or 'apps' and on smart phones. Another game, *Tetris*, a block-stacking puzzle from 1984, has been determined by a long study (by the University of San Francisco which scans players' brains at the addictive level), that has inspired new games to treat attention deficit disorder, depression, and other ills. Neuroimaging techniques are being used to call what scientists call "building better brains."

Sales at hobby stores in the USA have risen from 15 to 2090, believe it or not, for table top games, exceeding the amount of money spent on video games ($52.1 versus $45.3 million). One game called *Robot Turtles* teaches children basic computer programming concepts without their realizing. The designer had targeted raising $25,000 to get the game into production, but instead there was so much interest that $631,000 came in. *Cards against Humanity*, a profane and humorous game pairing noun and adjective words is another hit. "Euro" games emphasize strategy and compete for scarce resources, has been a success, and videogame players are amongst the strongest fans of tabletop games where face-to-face contact (lost with videogames) is deemed desirable!

A driving game from 2013 where players identify specific road signs while ignoring irrelevant ones, has been determined to help memory and attention. Shooter games studied by neuroscientists at the University of Rochester, NY have been seen to improve visual attention, decision making and reasoning after just two weeks

158

of play. Older people are helped, it is said, by a simple game called *Neuro Racer.*

Surgeons doing laparoscopic operations found, in a study at Iowa State University, to be 27% faster and make 37% fewer mistakes than non-players. Had you even considered the quantity of mistakes? The addictive point is being studied to go on from there.

Walmart stores (America's largest retail company) have offered to give store credit for old video games which they refurbish and distribute. This may be a threat to Game Stop, the largest retailer and the biggest seller of used games, which now has a 44 % market profit that came to $1.6 billion in 2013.

A 20 year old company in South Korea, Nexon, had more than $1.5 billion in revenue in 2013. Nexon pioneered a way for their on-lime games by letting players pay gratis but with opportunities to spend money on incidentals. Their premium model has entered into the game businesses from China and the West.

Owen Mahoney is chief executive of Nexon. Mahoney, who speaks fluent Japanese, moved Nexon headquarters to Japan after listing the shares on the Japanese Stock Market. Recently, 93% of Nexon's revenue came from China, Korea, and Japan. To make the Nexon games more appealing to Westerners, repetitive tasks will be modified. Westerners like their warriors to have neck and body tattoos, while the Japanese only allow this for gangsters.

In the gaming industry, success has always been unpredictable. A huge fad, *Candy Crush*, is an addictive mobile game, which has been downloaded half a billion times. The game belongs to an Irish company called King Digital Entertainment. They made $567 million in profit on this game alone. Although the company has more than 100 games, 80% of their profits come from *Candy Crush.* The King Company had only $7.8 million in 2012, until they hit this winner. But the unpredictability of the game world can flip in the other direction. Such huge games such as *Guitar Hero* and *Rock Band* faded quickly. A single designer created *Flappy Bird*, a hugely successful game in just a few days. *Flappy bird* has been downloaded 50 million times in just a couple of weeks. However, the popular app was withdrawn by its creator as addictive and without cognitive improvement merits.

"Permadeath" equipped with weapons inspired by Star Trek, complete with a starship and shields, has been coined to describe games where a death has real importance and leads to irreversible consequences. A game called *Faster than Light*, inspired by Star Trek, complete with a starship and shields, won an excellence in design award at the 2013's Independent Games Festival. The game is very difficult and full of tension as the player is on the run from powerful enemies.

As of January 2013, the New York Film Academy offers a Game Design B.A. and Masters Degree. The courses, located in the back lot of Universal Studios in Hollywood can be taken even if the student is in Australia, China, Japan, the Middle East, Paris or Florence. Students make video games that tie into the video game industry. With potentially huge profits at stake, video game companies are vying to create the next 'must-have' game.

Online games are growing phenomenally. The number of internet users in the USA playing games at least every month reached 27% of the population in 2011. At least 60 million Americans have played a game on a social network, and it is said that this trend has just begun. These games are now organized into three categories: multi-player online, role-playing games such as *World of Warcraft* or *Clash of Clans*, and life and style games such as *The Sims*. France is using *Cyber Budget*, an online game that asks players to manage France's budget issues.

A game called *Of War: Fire Age* was designed to have players around the world play simultaneously with instant translations of players' online 'chat'. The massive multi-player game has more than eight million subscribers. The competition is worldwide and aimed to intensify both competition and communication between the players. Every player's location is featured on a single map, and the software comes in many languages, so that everyone in the world can play the same game together and all at once (a world war)!

An Austrian group of web developers have introduced an animated cartoon game called *Data Dealer* in which players are encouraged to amass and sell fictional consumer profiles including personal data, birth dates, consumer activities, etc. Each player begins with five thousand dollars in credit and a database. Real names then replace pseudonyms and players can sell their profiles to the game endeavoring to explain and alert the players to the value of various profiles.[2]

A game entitled *Darfur is Dying* had seven hundred thousand players, of which tens of thousands signed petitions and e-mailed politicians to intervene in the Darfur crisis. The popular social network game, *Farmville*, incorporated fundraising for Haitian earthquake victims into its game. People feel part of a team, an element of play. Was play ever expected to be like this?

The passion for games and gambling has lasted despite the vast choice of other entertainments and distractions now available. Mahjong parlors, either temporary or permanent (when the police don't find them and close them down), are numerous in Chinatowns across the USA. If the house does not take a commission, then it is not illegal. Street gangs had a strong hold on the mahjong parlors in the 1990s until law enforcement broke them up. Some of the parlors are also used for lotteries and high stake card games, and sometimes have electronic gambling machines such as those in Las Vegas. Mahjong parlors became a key source of income for certain districts and family organizations in Chinatown.

From Macao to Las Vegas casinos all over the world are going strong. More than $1 billion of bets are known to be placed per year just in the United States. Casinos routinely give rewards for steady patronage such as free hotel nights, meals, appliances, and even dressing gowns.

Gambling opportunities are multiplying, as it is now legal throughout America (with the exception, still in 2013, of Hawaii and Utah). In-state gambling is legal in some states, but gambling across state lines would require a change in federal law. States can set up gambling facilities in order to increase state revenue. It was recently reported in the *New York Times* that a small town in Colorado was building a casino in hopes of increasing revenue for their colleges and reversing the negative effects of the global economic recession on state-funded schools. In 2006 eleven casino licenses were issued in

[2] Federal US Regulators have been urging data users to make their practices more transparent to protect consumers' privacy.

Pennsylvania for the first time. In the state of Massachusetts, three new resort-style casinos and a slot parlor were licensed, a monopoly that had previously been held by Native Americans.

Since 2011, the Obama Administration approved five Indian reservation casinos. This opened a new wave of tribal battles across the country. In Arizona, two tribes have held up a project due to their many lawsuits. In Wisconsin, a tribe which has approval already for a casino outside of Milwaukee has competition from other tribes, particularly the Seminole of Florida, as the Wisconsin tribe has only 9000 souls and is the poorest in the state. The Seminole tribe owns seven casinos, (but without roulette or craps) featuring *jai alai* and poker, as well as Greyhound race tracks. The Seminole have exclusive rights to table games and pay $5 billion to the state of Florida each year.

The Seminoles have also contributed financially to all political parties in the prospect of operating the casinos. In California, the opponents to the North Forks Casino have donated more than $2 million. The Chukchansi and Table Mountain tribes have allied themselves with a group that believes that the state could become overrun with off-reservation casinos, such as proposed by the North Fork Project.

Indian Tribes in California without land are seeking to open a casino only 30 miles from that of another tribe. They have turned, for the first time, to the voters to keep newcomers off their turf. There are 109 Indian tribes and more than 60 casinos already. There are six additional tribes applying to open new casinos and 78 new groups applying for federal tribe recognition, a prerequisite for a casino. Tribes with land far from urban areas are buying closer to cities in the hopes of opening casinos.

A front page headline on August 1, 2013 in the *New York Times* stated that while a record 39.7 million visitors went to Las Vegas in 2012, the total revenue from gambling and entertainment other than gambling was $15.3 billion, $300 billion less than was spent in 2007. Whether this was the result of the weakened economy or because Las Vegas has now become just one of many gambling destinations in the United States, is not yet known. Las

Vegas hotelier and casino owner Steve Wynn has opened a major casino on a 52-acre parcel of land in Macau with a hotel and 450 gambling tables. Steve Wynn says that he sees a big problem in not allowing casino operators to keep the money. Macau now has the highest revenue from gambling in the world.

The Chinese, who were always great gamblers, including the workers on the railroad from California to Utah in the 1860's, created a community by gambling. Little round pellets that they used have been unearthed in work camp sites in British Columbia. Now their popular games are dice games called "*da-xiao*" (big-little), as well as roulette. Roulette and baccarat (played in Macau) are the most popular games there.

Macau, the former Portuguese colony in south China, as a gambling Mecca, dwarfs Las Vegas. It has a Grand Canal, complete with a Rialto bridge, and an Eiffel tower and a resort modeled on the palace of Versailles. $3.9 billion complex is scheduled to open in 2017 with 700 gambling tables and hotels called Pilazzo, Versace, and another hotel designed by Karl Lagerfeld.

Gambling revenues in Macau have soared to approximately $46 billion last year, whereas Las Vegas generated $6.5 billion in 2013, with little growth. The American casino operator mentioned before, Wynn Resorts, is planning a 1700 room and casino complex in Macau, although taxes are much higher than in Las Vegas. One in five Chinese who went beyond mainland china, (where gambling is prohibited), went to Macau in 2013. A bridge is being built between Hong Kong and Macau to be ready in 2016. Analysts have forecast that gambling revenue there could double by 2018.

Chinese gamblers risk a motorcycle ride through a rebel-held jungle to get to Myanmar (formerly Burma) going through holes in the border fence to avoid the official border crossing, despite insurgents demanding payoffs en route. The region is controlled by a Warlord with thousands of armed men who co-exist with the ethnic Ma militia and government forces. Mong La, the gamblers' destination, had been the site where Chinese officials gambled (with stolen public money), causing soldiers to be dispatched, and was the inspiration to build new casinos ten miles into the jungle. Permits required to cross the Myanmar border legally are designed to limit visitors from Beijing, but the permits are hardly applied for. Signs are also posted forbidding Chinese citizens from entering the casinos which are filled, nevertheless, almost entirely by Chinese players.

The majority of the residents and almost all the clients of the twenty Chinese-owned casinos are Chinese. China also provides electricity and phone service, as well as having Chinese money the currency accepted at the casinos. When, in 2012, cell phone service was severed in an attempt to stop Internet gambling, the casino owners installed satellite dishes to continue their operations from Shanghai and other Chinese cities. In the casinos, scores play hands with remote Chinese gamblers on headsets through remote video feeds.

Loan sharks are everywhere. Gamblers with huge losses (single bets can be over $30,000) are precluded from returning home as the lenders do not allow a borrower to leave unless all is paid up.

A Myanmar gambling center called Mong La has a large market also for endangered wildlife for culinary and other uses, with over forty rare breeds (including animals which have been believed extinct). Elephant tusks are also for sale in huge quantity. Pornography, prostitution, handguns, crystal meth, and stolen cars are all at hand and readily available- a really "delightful" destination.

New York State has approved the expansion of gambling in a vote on November 4, 2013. The gambling industry's long and expensive effort to break into New York, promoted by a group called "New York Jobs" is, in fact financed by gambling interests with a budget of $4 million. The gambling centers will be located mostly in upstate New York and in areas near the northern border of Pennsylvania. Recently, opposition to the expansion of gambling facilities in Saratoga Springs has surprised proponents of expanded gambling in upstate New York.[3]

The competition has grown and is projected to become bitter, regarding plans (begun in the 1970's) to build a $500 million casino resort in upstate New York. Newcomers wishing to build casinos only 49 miles from

[3]   Jesse McKinley (Jan. 12, 2014) "Upstate Opposition to a Casino is a Surprise" *The New York Times.* Retrieved from http://www.nytimes.com/2014/01/13/nyregion/upstate-opposition-to-a-casino-is-a-surprise.html?_r=0

New York, (instead of the 99 miles location originally proposed) are trying to get their projects approved. Other casino developers further away from New York City are protesting, as the casinos closer to the city would also cut off their patrons. The further upstate communities have higher unemployment, few job prospects, are the neediest, and are supported by the governor to be the chosen site for the new casinos to revitalize the local economy. All of this creates very high stakes, and even before the games begin!

A developer called David Flaun, and his son, from Rochester New York, has purchased four sites from Albany to Orange County to compete for licenses for upstate New York. One of their sites is near a mall that attracts 11 million visitors per year and only 15 miles from New York City. The argument against this site is that the legislation against legalizing casino building was enacted to counteract high unemployment and low income upstate. The Flauns have been large donors to both democratic and republican parties.

The Caesars Entertainment Company operates 53 casinos worldwide. They have sent their million dollar application for the casino license, which they would like to have built in Orange County, about an hour from New York City. They are planning to spend $750 million dollars on whatever they build. There are complaints that an Orange County Casino would siphon business away from existing slot callers. Other casino companies are interested in even closer counties to New York City. As for proposals for casinos in the Catskills, to quote Charles Jacobs of the Cordish Companies, "It would be a recipe for disaster," as it would trump potential casinos in New York State, which the governor believes are much more needed for alleviating unemployment and the low upstate tax revenues. Debate over the bids for the casinos will be intense. The formal dues are due June 30th of 2014, and the decisions should be made in the autumn.

Another group, the Genting, operates Resorts World slot parlors at the aqueduct track in Queens and multi-billion dollar resorts in Asia, and is particularly interested building in the Catskills and Hudson Valley regions, but their prime interest is in Tuxedo, New York, which is only

40 miles from midtown New York City. They, too, have sent in their $1 million application for a license. The Saratoga Albany Region and a narrow strip of western New York State, reaching the Canadian border, are also available for casino building. Some believe the market is already saturated with existing slot parlors from Rhode Island down to Maryland. There are already five Indian Casinos upstate and slot machines that run at nine race-tracks.

The newly-created New York State Gaming Commission will charge $1 million not refundable, just to apply for a gaming casino. The license itself will cost up to $70 million in orange or Duchess Counties, and half that in the Catskills, or up to $50 million. There then will be hundreds of millions of dollars to build the casinos, for which there are already 22 contestants. A billionaire casino owner, Sheldon Adelson, has paid huge amounts to many politicians and lobbyists. Mr. Adelson is seeking to outlaw eventual online gambling, which has divided Washington's powerful interests groups. He has paid over $100 million into republican coffers in the last three years over an old loophole in federal law banning online gambling, which he believes would harm their casino businesses. Mr. Adelson has threatened to withdraw from the American Gaming Association, which backed expanding online gambling and has bankrolled the coalition to stop internet gambling. The group includes former governor of New York, George Pataki, who has presided over a huge expansion in New York which includes online betting on horse races.

Online gambling has long been illegal, but in 2011, the justice department allowed individual states to permit it as a lucrative source of revenue for them. The fight is, as usual, all about money. A company, AAA, is to begin a project again for a $billion + entertainment and shopping center in the New Jersey meadowlands, only five miles west of Manhattan, which will include an indoor water park, skydiving, Ferris wheels, and an amusement park, all connected with gambling.

A billionaire, *KTLIN*, whose company operates the *RESORT WORLD* Slot Parlors aqueduct racetrack in Queens, as well as multibillion dollar resorts in Asia, is a heavy contributor to both republican and democratic parties with multiple lobbyists employed in New York State.

Bidders have donated $55 million so far to the N.Y state governor and his likely republican opponent had received $43,000 for his reelection last year as a Westchester County executive. N.Y State reaped $200 million in license fees this year alone. The decisions are supposed to be politically neutral. For licenses granted, taxes are steep: 45% of gross revenue from slot machines and 10% from craps and roulette. The capital investments required to open a casino could rise to $1 billion or more in the areas near N.Y City.

The media has brought the issue of gambling addiction to light. Support groups such as *Gamblers Anonymous* attest to its recognition as an addiction.[4] A former Mayor of San Diego, spent almost ten years gambling, losing $1 billion at casinos. She had to sell all her possessions, a luxury hotel and real estate, and stole two million dollars from a charitable foundation. It was calculated that she must have been betting more than three hundred dollars per day for seven days a week over her nine to ten year gambling career.

The elderly are a particularly vulnerable demographic for pathological gambling. The older gambler is 0.8% at risk for pathological betting (compared to 0.5% of all adult gamblers). A study by the Florida Council on Compulsive Gambling discovered that 6-9% of the state's population were at risk for problem gambling. Despite the national explosion in gambling, the percentage of pathological gamblers in the United States is said to have remained under one percent since the 1970s.

Despite its corporatization, gambling is still associated with local criminality. In December 2007, New Jersey police reportedly broke up an organized crime ring involving the Lucchese mob which had taken an estimated $2.2 billion in gambling bets in a single year.[5] The position of governments in respect to gambling profits and winnings varies. Private gambling was formerly non-taxable in most of the Commonwealth countries but that is beginning to change. The Australian government, for example, has sued mathematical savant David Walsh for

[4]   Several movies with this theme appeared in 2007 in the United States such as *The Grand, Lucky You,* and *Even Money.* The movies focuses on compulsive gambling among middle to upper class Americans.

[5]   "Reputed Lucchese Mob Ring Broken Up in New Jersey" http://wcbstv. com (18 December 2007)

retrospective taxes on his gambling winnings, asking for $40 million plus interest. Until now, the courts have ruled in favor of the gambler.

Off-track betting parlors are planning to update their facilities to expand it customer bases. While gambling in New York City is increasing, the outdated quarters for off-track betting have been a deterrent. These establishments are trying to entice younger gamblers and "break down the barriers," (as the president of the New York City Off-Track Betting Cooperation puts it), "that exist for people to try sports racing." For instance, during the Belmont Stakes a giant video screen was set up in Times Square in New York with customer service representatives dressed as jockeys. The betting corporation is also planning to bring betting computers to more expensive restaurants.

The first casino in New York City, which can conveniently be reached by subway from Times Square, has opened in the borough of Queens. This enormous space features five thousand video gambling terminals and electronic table games, including craps and a popular Asian dice game called *sic bo*. The casino is owned by Resorts World, a subsidiary of a Malaysian company that operates in Britain and Southeast Asia. There are 35,000 visitors a day and over 12 million visitors a year. The baccarat table will have real cards, which will be shuffled and dealt by robots (human dealers are not permitted by New York State gambling laws). The closing time at the casino is four a.m., seven days a week. Critics say the casino comes close to breaching constitutional gambling limits.

The United States Justice Department reversed their decision opposing internet gambling, in late December 2011. Within a state, gambling online will now be legal except for bets on sporting events. The law that had made gambling over telecommunications systems (crossing state or national lines) illegal prevented states from using the internet to sell lottery tickets. The decision specifically dealt with lottery tickets and may now open the way to allow internet poker and other betting that does not involve sporting events.

Many states that desperately need additional revenue are satisfied with the new filing to allow online gambling.

In New York, lottery officials are planning two additional jackpot games, while also allowing NY residents to buy single-draw tickets online. With credit card purchases, the state can also guard and monitor against excessive play. It has been estimated that internet gambling could bring from six to one hundred billion dollars to the states.

It is estimated that the world will be betting $100 billion by 2017 on mobile devices alone. Bill Eadington, long time Director of the Institute for the Study of Gambling and Commercial Gaming at the University of Nevada, noted that gambling can be a force for economic development and challenging social problems. Online gambling, although a popular idea with millions of Americans is still illegal in the United States, and the casino industry considers it a threat. A trade group that represents major casinos such as Wynn resorts, MGM Resorts and Harrah's Entertainment, along with the American Gaming Association, is proposing, however, that Congress legalize some form of online gambling. They propose that, properly-regulated online gambling should be limited to poker. Casinos make only 2% of their revenue from poker.

In 2013, the USA doubled the lottery ticket price to two dollars. With a jackpot of $40 million, the Multi-State Lottery Association predicts that fifteen million people will buy tickets. According to another entity, the North American Association of State and Provincial Lotteries (which represents two lottery groups) reports that nineteen billion dollars was returned to the states that sponsored the lotteries. A caveat: unless the jackpot is more that $75 million, it wouldn't be worth playing as state and federal taxes would take about half the winnings. To quote an anonymous professor of mathematics, the odds are "175 million to one against you."

A *Quick Draw* Lottery game has been played in small shops since its introduction to New York in 1995. The governor is now proposing to eliminate restrictions as to where the game can be played. The new ruling would allow play in restaurants, bowling alleys, bars, and large stores. The players' age is a point of dispute, (playing is not allowed where liquor is served). The game already generates $138 million per year for the New York State Education budget. In *Quick Draw*, players match numbers on a ticket generated by computer. The game has been called "video crack," because it rivals slot machines in its addictive potential. An MIT anthropologist wrote that players of such games become addicted three to four times faster than with other forms of gambling.[6] A recent article in the New York Times pointed out the social crises ensuing from the popularity of easily accessible slot machines, especially in Northern Italy, where, in the province of Pavia, household expenditure on gambling has reached more than 4,000 Euros annually.[7] Italy is now Europe's largest gambling market, and fourth worldwide, following the U.S., Japan, and Macau.[8]

[6] Books recently published about the danger of computer addiction include *The Distraction Addiction* by Alex Soojung-Kim Pang (Little, Brown & Co.), *The App Generation* by Howard Gardner and Katie Davis (Yale University Press) and *The Big Disconnect* by Catherine Steine-Adeir with Teresa Barker (Harper).

[7] Elisabetta Povoledo (Dec. 28, 2013) "Fears of Social Breakdown as Gambling Explodes in Italy" in The New York Times. Retrieved from http://www.nytimes.com/2013/12/29/world/europe/fears-of-social-breakdown-as-gambling-explodes-in-italy.html

[8] Elisabetta Povoledo (Dec. 28, 2013) "Fears of Social Breakdown as Gambling Explodes in Italy" in The New York Times. Retrieved from http://www.nytimes.com/2013/12/29/world/europe/fears-of-social-breakdown-as-gambling-explodes-in-italy.html

"Go out and play? What is this, 1962?"

The New Yorker (September 13, 2013)

BIBLIOGRAPHY

Addobbati, Andrea. *La festa e il gioco nella Toscana del Settecento*. Pisa: Plus, 2002.

Alberti, Leon Battista. *I libri della famiglia, Cena familiaris, Villa*. Bari: G. Laterza, 1960.

Alexander, John T. *Catherine the Great: Life & Legend*. New York, Oxford: Oxford University Press, 1989.

Almanach du Trou-Madame: jeu très-ancien et très-connu, et la cause de presque toutes les révolutions. Paris: Chez Chuchet, Librarie, rue & Hôtel Serpente, 1791.

Ariès, Philippe, and Georges Duby, gen. eds. *A History of Private Life, Vol. II: Revelations of the Medieval World*. Trans. by Arthur Goldhammer. Cambridge, MA, London: Belknap Press of Harvard University Press, 1993.

Ariès, Philippe, and Georges Duby, gen. eds. *A History of Private Life, Vol. III: Passions of the Renaissance*. Trans. by Arthur Goldhammer. Cambridge, MA, London: Belknap Press of Harvard University Press, 1989.

Arnaldi, Girolamo and Manlio Pastore Stocchi, eds. *Storia della cultura veneta, III.1, Dal primo Quattrocento al concilio di Trento*. Vicenza: N. Pozza, 1976.

Art du jeu, jeu dans l'Art. De Babylone à l'Occident médiéval. Exh. cat., Musée de Cluny, 2012-2013. Paris: Réunion des musées nationaux-Grand Palais, 2012.

St. Augustine. *De civitate Dei contra paganos*. Bk. iv. Praeceptorio. Cons. ed. Augustine, Saint, Bishop of Hippo. *The City of God by Saint Augustine*. Transl. by Marcus Dods. New York: Modern Library, 1983.

Backman, Clifford R. *The Worlds of Medieval Europe*. New York: Oxford University Press, 2003.

Badinter, Elisabeth. *Mme du Châtelet, Mme d'Epinay ou L'ambition féminine au XVIII siècle*. 2nd ed. Paris: Flammarion, 2006.

Baldwin, David. *Elizabeth Woodville: Mother of the Princes in the Tower*. Stroud, Gloucestershire: Sutton, 2002.

Beckford, William. *Italy. With Sketches of Spain and Portugal. By the author of "Vathek"*. London: R. Bentley, 1834.

Beltrami, Daniele. *Storia della popolazione di Venezia dalla fine del secolo XVI alla caduta della Repubblica*. Padova: CEDAM, 1954.

Bernardino da Siena. *Prediche volgari sul Campo di Siena, 1427*. Edited by Carlo Delcorno. 2 vols. Milano: Rusconi, 1989.

Bernis, François-Joachim de Pierres, cardinal de. *Mémoires du cardinal de Bernis*. Paris: Mercure de France, 1986.

Bobbitt, Philip. *The Garments of Court and Palace. Machiavelli and the World That He Made*. New York: Grove Press, 2013.

Boccaccio, Giovanni. *Decamerone*. Vinegia: Johannes and Gregorius de Gregoriis, de Forlivio, 1492.

Boigne, Éléonore-Adèle d'Osmond, comtesse de. *Mémoires de la Comtesse de Boigne I du regne de Louis XVI à 1820*. 2 vols. Paris: Mercure de France, 1999.

Borst, Arno. *Forme di vita nel Medioevo*. Napoli: Guida, 1988.

Brizay, François. *Touristes du Grand Siècle. Le voyage d'Italie au XVIIe siècle*. Paris: Belin, 2006.

Brosses, Charles de. *Le Président de Brosses en Italie. Lettres familières écrites d'Italie en 1739 et 1740*. 2 vols. Paris: Les Editions Didier, 1858.

Bryson, Bill. *At Home: A Short History of Private Life*. New York: Doubleday, 2010.

Burckhardt, Jacob. *The Civilization of the Renaissance in Italy*. Trans. by S.G.C. Middlemore. 1860. Reprint, London: Penguin, 2004.

Burke, Peter. *The Italian Renaissance. Culture and Society in Italy*. Princeton NJ: Princeton University Press, 1999.

Calasso, Roberto. *Il rosa Tiepolo*. Milano: Adelphi, 2006.

Campan, Madame de. *Mémoires de Madame Campan, première femme de chambre de Marie Antoinette*. 1788. Reprint, Paris: Mercure de France, 1988.

Campion, Henri de. *Mémoires de Henri de Campion, suivis de trois entretiens sur divers sujets d'histoire, de politique et de morale...* Edited by Marc Fumaroli. Paris: Mercure de France, 1967.

Carré, Lt.-Col. Henri. *La Duchesse de Bourgogne. Une princesse de Savoie à la cour de Louis XIV, 1685–1712*. Paris: Hachette, 1934.

Carrera, Pietro. *Il gioco de gli scacchi*. 1617. Reprint, Catania: Comune di Militello in Val di Catania, 2003.

Casanova de Seingalt, Jacques. *Histoire de ma vie. Mémoires, suivie de textes inédits*. 3 vols. Paris: R. Laffont, 1993.

Castiglione, Baldassare. *Il libro del Cortegiano, con una scelta delle opere minori*. Edited by Bruno Maier. 2nd edition. Torino: UTET, 1964.

Cavalcanti, Giovanni. *Istorie fiorentine*. c. 1420s. Edited by Guido Di Pino. Milano: Martello, 1944.

Caylus, Marthe-Marguerite Le Valois de Villette de Murçay, comtesse de.

Souvenirs de Mme de Caylus. Edited by Bernard Nöel. Paris: Mercure de France, 1986.

Chekhov, Anton Pavlovich. *A Life in Letters.* Transl. and edited by Gordon McVay. London: Penguin Classics, 2004.

Chess, East & West, Past & Present. Exh. cat., New York, The Metropolitan Museum of Art, 1968. Wilkinson, Charles K. and Jessie McNab-Dennis eds. New York: The Metropolitan Museum of Art, 1968.

Chiomenti Vassalli, Donata. *Donna Olimpia o del nepotismo nel Seicento.* Milano: Mursia, 1979.

Choiseul, Étienne-François de. *Mémoires du duc de Choiseul.* Paris: Mercure de France, 1987.

Cohen, Thomas V. *Love and Death in Renaissance Italy.* Chicago: University of Chicago Press, 2004.

Cortesi, Santa, ed. *I due testamenti di Fra Sabba da Castiglione.* Faenza: Stefano Casanova, 2000.

Cotton, Charles. *The Complete Gamester.* London: Henry Brome, 1674.

Dangeau, Philippe de Courcillon, marquis de. *Journal, Volumes I-X.* Paris: Librairie de Firmin Didot Frères, 1854.

Daschkova, Ekaterina Romanovna, Princess. *Memoirs of the Princess Daschkaw, Lady of Honour to Catherine II, Empress of all the Russias; Letters of the Empress and other Correspondence. Vol. II.* Edited from the originals, by Mrs. W. Bradford. London: Henry Colburn, Publisher, Great Marlborough Street, 1840.

De Moivre, Abraham. *The Doctrine of Chances: or, a Method of Calculating the Probability of Events in Play.* London: W. Pearson, 1738.

Des Houlières, Antoinette. *Poésies. Réflexions sur le jeu.* Paris: chez la Veuve de Sébastien Mabre-Cramoisy, imprimeur du Roy, rue Saint Jacques, aux Cicognes, 1688.

Dixon, Simon. *Catherine the Great.* New York: Ecco, 2010.

Dolcetti, Giovanni. *Le Bische e il giuoco d'azzardo a Venezia. 1172-1807.* Venezia: Libreria Aldo Manuzio, 1903.

Du Hausset, Nicole. *Mémoires de Madame du Hausset sur Louis XV et Madame de Pompadour.* Edited by Quentin Craufurd. Paris: Mercure de France, 1985.

Dulong, Claude. *La Vie quotidienne des femmes au Grand Siècle.* Paris: Hachette, 1984.

Fallow, James. *The Atlantic Monthly:* vol. 299, September 2007.

Feltham, Owen. *Resolves. Divine, Morall, Politicall.* London: printed for H. Seile, 1623.

Fiorelli, Piero. *La tortura giudiziaria nel diritto comune.* 2 vols. [Milano]: Giuffré, 1953-54.

Fiorin, Alberto, ed. *Fanti e denari. Sei secoli di gioco d'azzardo.* Venezia: Arsenale Editrice, 1989.

Forbin, Claude de. *Mémoires du comte de Forbin. 1656–1733.* Paris: Mercure de France, 1993.

Foreman, Amanda. *Georgiana: Duchess of Devonshire.* New York, Modern Library, 2001.

La France romane au temps des premiers Capétiens (987-1152). Catalogue de l'éxposition (Louvre, 2005), sous la direction de Danielle Gaborit-Chopin. Paris: Éditions du Musée di Louvre, 2005.

Fumaroli, Marc. *Quand l'Europe parlait Français.* Paris: éd. de Fallois, 2001.

Gamer, Helena M. "The Earliest Evidence of Chess in Western Literature. The Einsiedeln Verses." *Speculum,* vol. 29, 4, Oct., 1954: 734-750.

Geoffroy de Charny. *Le livre de chevalerie.* In: Jean Froissart, Burke, Peter. *The Italian Renaissance. Culture and Society in Italy.* Princeton NJ: Princeton University Press, 1999. *Œuvres de Froissart,* ed. Kervyn de Lettenhove, 25 vols., Bruxelles: V. Devaux, 1870-77, I, part III, 1873: 463-533.

Godolphin, Francis Richard Borroum, ed. *The Greek Historians. The complete and unabridged historical works of Herodotus.* New York: Random House, [1942].

Goldberg, Edward L. *Patterns in Late Medici Art Patronage.* Princeton, NJ: Princeton University Press, 1983.

Goldoni, Carlo. *Mémoires de M. Goldoni.* Paris: Vve Duchesne, 1787.

Goldoni, Carlo. "Una delle ultime sere di Carnovale. Commedia allegorica di tre atti in prosa. Rappresentata per la prima volta in Venezia nel carnovale dell'anno 1761", in *Commedie buffe in prosa del sig. Carlo Goldoni:* in *Opere teatrali del sig. avvocato Carlo Goldoni veneziano: con rami allusive,* 47 vols. Venezia: dalle stampe di Antonio Zatta e figli, 1788-1795, XXXIV, T. 12, 1793, A c. A3r.

Goldthwaite, Richard A. *The Building of Renaissance Florence.* Baltimore and London: Johns Hopkins University Press, 1980.

Goodman, Martin. *Rome and Jerusalem: The Clash of Ancient Civilizations.* New York: Vintage Books, 2008.

Guiffrey, Jules, ed. *Inventaires de Jean, duc de Berry.* 2 vols. Paris: E. Leroux, 1894–1896.

Giuntella, Vittorio E. *Roma nel Settecento.* Bologna: Cappelli, 1971.

Hailes, David Darlymple, Lord, ed. *The Opinions of Sarah Duchess-Dowager of Marlborough.* Edinburgh: s.n., 1788.

Hale, Sheila. *Titian: His Life.* London: HarperPress, 2012.

Halsband, Robert. *The Life of Lady Mary Wortley Montagu,* Vol. II. Oxford: Clarendon Press, 1956.

Hammond, Alex. *The Book of Chessmen.* London: Arthur Barker, 1950.

Hargrave, Catherine Perry. *History of Playing Cards and a Bibliography of Cards and Gaming.* New York: Dover Publications: 1966.

Herbert, George. *Jacula Prudentum; or Outlandish Proverbs, Sentences, &c. Selected by Mr. George Herbert.* 2nd edition. London: Printed by T. Maxey for T. Garthwait…, 1651.

Honour, Hugh. *The Companion Guide to Venice.* Melton, Woodbridge, Suffolk: Boydell & Brewer Ltd, 1965.

Jacques de Cessoles. *Le livre du jeu d'échecs.* Transl. and edited by Jean-Michel Mehl. Paris: Stock, 1995.

Jefferson, Thomas. *Letter to Martha Jefferson,* Marseille, May 21, 1787 <http://www.let.rug.nl/usa/presid

ents/thomas-jefferson/letters-of-thomas-jefferson/jefl58.php>.

Le Jeu au XVIIIe Siecle. Aix-en-Provence: Edisud, 1967.

John of Salisbury, *Policraticus, Book I.* [1175]. Ed. and trans. Cary Nederman. Cambridge: Cambridge University Press, 1990.

Juegos diversos de axedrez, dados y tablas con sus explicaciones, ordenados por mandado del rey don Alfonso el Sabio. Facsimile edition. Códigos I.G. de la Biblioteca del Escorial. Madrid-Valencia: Ediciones Poniente y Vincent García Editores, 1987.

Keats, Victor A. *Chess in Jewish History and Hebrew Literature.* Jerusalem: Magnes Press, 1995.

Keighley, Thomas. *Secret Societies of the Middle Ages.* London: s.n., 1837.

Kelly, Ian. *Cooking for Kings. The Life of Antonin Carême, the First Celebrity Chef.* New York: Walker & Co., 2003.

Kelly, John. *The Great Mortality. An Intimate History of the Black Death, the Most Devastating Plague of All Time.* New York: Harper Collins, 2005.

King, Ross. *Michelangelo and the Pope's Ceiling.* London: Pimlico, 2003.

Kingsford, C.L. "John de Bensted and his Missions for Edward I." *Essays in History Presented to Reginald Lane Poole.* Ed. H.W.C. Davis. Oxford: Clarendon Press, 1929.

Lacombe, Jacques. *Encyclopédie methodique. Dictionnaire des jeux avec les planches relatives, faisant suite aux amusemens des sciences mathemathiques & c.* A Padoue, s.n., 1800.

La Guette, Catherine de. *Mémoires de Madame de la Guette 1613–1676, écrits par elle-même.* Edited by Micheline Cuénin. Reprint. Paris: Mercure de France, 1982.

Lamb, Charles, "Mrs. Battle's Opinion on Whist." *Elia. Essays Which Have Appeared under that Signature in the London Magazine.* London: s.n., 1823

Laven, Mary. *Virgins of Venice. Broken Vows and Cloistered Life in the Renaissance Convent.* New York: Viking Press, 2003.

Lewis, Bernard. *The Middle East: A Brief History of the Last 2,000 Years.* New York, London: Scribner, 1995.

Liddell, Donald M. *Chessmen.* New York: Harcourt, Brace & Co., 1937.

Ligne, Charles Joseph, prince de. *Mémoires du Prince de Ligne: suivis de pensées et précédés d'une introduction.* Paris-Bruxelles: A. Bohné, Van Meenen, 1860.

Lister, Dr. Martin. *A Journey to Paris in the Year 1698.* London: s.n., 1699.

Lough, John. *France on the Eve of Revolution: British Travellers' Observations 1763-1788.* London: Croom Helm, 1987.

Machiavelli, Niccolò. *La Mandragola.* Fiorenza: appresso i Giunti, 1556.

Mackett-Beeson, Alfred Ernest James. *Chessmen.* London: Octopus Books, 1973.

Manchester, William. *A World Lit Only by Fire: The Medieval Mind and the Renaissance, Portrait of an Age.* Boston, New York, London: Little Brown & Co., 1992.

Marguerite de Valois. "Les temps d'epreuves – Lettres d'epreuves." *Mémoires de Marguerite de Valois.* Paris: Mercure de France, 1742.

Marguerite de Valois. *Mémories et autres écrits de Marguerite de Valois, la reine Margot.* Ed. by Yves Cazaux. Paris: Mercure de France, 1971.

Marozzi, Justin. *Tamerlane: Sword of Islam, Conqueror of the World.* London: Harper Collins, 2004.

Martines, Lauro. *April Blood: Florence and the Plot Against the Medici.* London: Jonathan Cape, 2003.

Mee, Charles L., jr. *The Horizon Book of Daily Life in Renaissance Italy.* New York: American Heritage Publishing Co., 1975.

Mehl, Jean-Michel. *Les jeux au royaume de France du XIIIe au début du XVIe siècle.* Paris: Fayard, 1990.

Misson, François Maximilien. *A New Voyage to Italy: with Curious Observations on Several Other Countries....* London: s.n., 1714.

Montpensier, Anne-Marie-Louise-Henriette d'Orléans, duchesse de. *La grande Mademoiselle: Mémoires de 1627 à 1643.* Edited by Chantal Thomas. Paris: Mercure de France, 2001.

Murray, Harold James Ruthven. *A History of Chess.* Oxford: Clarendon Press, 1913.

Nelson, Janet L. "Medieval Queenship." *Women in Medieval Western European Culture.* Linda E. Mitchell, ed. New York, London: Garland, 1999.

Nuridsany, Michel. *Ce será notre secret, Monsieur Watteau.* Paris: Flammarion, 2006.

Oberkirch, Henriette-Louise de Waldner de Freundstein, baronne d'. *Mémoires sur la cour de Louis XVI et la société française avant 1789.* Reprint, Paris: Mercure de France, 1989.

Orléans, Charlotte-Elisabeth de Bavière, duchesse d'. *Lettres de Madame, duchesse d'Orléans, née princesse Palatine.* Edited by Olivier Amiel. Paris: Mercure de France, 1999.

The Pilgrimage of Charlemagne. Aucassin and Nicolette. Glyn S. Burgess and Anne Elizabeth Cobby, eds. and transl. New York, London: Garland Press, 1988.

Philidor, François-André. *Analyse du jeu des échecs, par A.D. Philidor, édition augmentée de soixante-huit parties jouées par Philidor, du Traité de Greco, des Débuts de Stamma et de Ruy-Lopez, par C. Sanson,...* Paris: Garnier frères, 1873.

Phillips, Hubert and B.C. Westall. *The Complete Book of Card Games.* London: H.F & G. Witherby Ltd, 1939.

Pope, Alexander. *An Essay on Man, Being the First Book of Ethic epistles. To Henry St. John, L. Bolingbroke.* London: Printed by John Wright, for Lawton Gilliver, 1734.

"Reputed Lucchese Mob Ring Broken Up in New Jersey." <http://wcbstv.com.> 18 December 2007.

Reynaud, Élisabeth. *Madame Élisabeth, soeur de Louis XVI.* Paris: Ramsay, 2007.

Rheims, Maurice. *La vie étrange des objets. Histoire de la curiosité.* Paris: Plon, 1959.

Saint-Simon, Louis de Rouvroy, duc de. *Mémoires sur la Régence.* Francis

Kaplan ed. Paris: Flammarion, 2001.

Sanudo, Marino. *I diarii di Marino Sanuto*. Pubblicato per cura di Rinaldo Fulin. Venezia: a spese degli editori, 1880.

Savage, Alan. *Eleanor of Aquitaine: Queen & Legend*. Sutton: Severn House, 1995.

Savelli, Marcantonio. *Pratica Universale…*. In Venezia: presso Paolo Baglioni, 1707.

Scarne, John. *Scarne's Complete Guide to Gambling*. New York: Simon and Schuster, 1961.

The Secular Spirit: Life & Art at the End of the Middle Ages. Exh. cat., New York, The Cloisters, 1975. New York: Dutton, 1975.

Segneri, Paolo. *Lettera di Paolo Segneri della Compagnia di Giesu all'Illustriss. rever. sig. e padrone colendiss. monsignor n.n. su la materia del probabile*. Colonia: presso Baldassarre d'Egmond, 1703.

Sercambi, Giovanni. *Novelle*. Giovanni Sinicropi ed. Bari: Gius. Laterza & Figli, 1972.

Sévigné, Marie de Rabutin-Chantal, marquise de. *Correspondance. 2 (1675-1680)*. Edited by Roger Duchêne. Paris: Gallimard, 1986.

Snyder, Steven James. "Film Review." *The New York Sun*, May 16, 2007.

Specter, Michael. "Planet Kirsan." *The New Yorker*. 24 April 2006, p. 112–22.

Staël-Holstein, Anne-Louise-Germaine, baronne de. *Lettres sur les ouvrages et le caractère de J.-J. Rousseau*. [Paris]: Au Temple de la vertu, chez le premier restaurateur de la France, 1789.

Storie di viaggiatori italiani. 4 vols. Milano: Electa, 1985-88.

Suetonius. "The Deified Augustus." *Lives of the Caesars*. New York: Barnes & Noble, 2004.

Talleyrand-Périgord, Charles Maurice de, prince de Bénévent. *Memoirs…* 5 vols. London: Griffith & Farran, 1891-92.

Taylor, Francis Henry. *The Taste of Angels: A History of Art Collecting from Rameses to Napoleon*. Boston: Little, Brown and Co., 1948.

Thietmar, von Merseburg, Bishop of Merseburg. *Ottonian Germany: the Chronicon of Thietmar of Merseburg*. Translated and annotated by David A. Warner. Manchester: Manchester University Press, 2001.

Tilly, Alexandre de. *Mémoires du comte Alexandre de Tilly, pour servir à l'histoire des moeurs de la fin du XVIIIe siècle*. Edited by Christian Melchior-Bonnet. [Paris]: Mercure de France, 2003.

Tillyard, Stella K. *A Royal Affair: George III and His Scandalous Siblings*. New York: Random House, 2006.

Trexler, Richard C. *Public Life in Renaissance Florence*. Ithaca: Cornell University Press, 1991.

Tourzel, Louise Élisabeth de Croÿ d'Havré, duchesse de. *Mémoires de Madame la duchesse de Tourzel, gouvernante des enfants de France de 1789 à 1795*. Paris: Mercure de France, 2005.

Twiss, Richard. *Chess. [A compilation of anecdotes and quotations relative to the game]*. 2 vols. London: G.G.J. & J. Robinson; T. & J. Egerton, 1787-89

Unger, Miles J. *Magnifico: The Brilliant Life and Violent Times of Lorenzo de' Medici*. New York: Simon and Schuster, 2008.

Walker, James. "Gambling and Venetian Noblemen c. 1500-1700." *Past & Present*, 162, Feb., 1999: 28-69.

Walpole, Horace, sir. *Lord Oxford's Reminiscences*. London: John Sharpe, 1818.

Warner, Jessica. *Craze: Gin, and Debauchery in an Age of Reason. Consisting of a Tragicomedy in Three Acts in Which High and Low are Brought Together, Much to Their Mutual Discomfort…* London: Profile, 2003.

Weatherford, Jack M. *Genghis Khan and the Making of the Modern World*. New York: Crown, 2004.

Weiss, Elizabeth Green. *New York Sun*. 21 May 2007.

Welch, Evelyn. *Shopping in the Renaissance: Consumer Cultures in Italy 1400-1600*. New Haven, Conn., London: Yale University Press, 2005.

Wichmann Hans and Siegfried Wichmann. *Chess: The Story of Chesspieces from Antiquity to Modern Times*. London: Paul Hamlyn, 1964.

Wilhelmine Friederike Sophie, margrave de Bayreuth. *Mémoires de Frédérique Sophie Wilhelmine, margrave de Bayreuth, soeur de Frédéric le Grand, depuis 1706 jusqu'à 1742, écrits de sa main*. Paris: Mercure de France, 1967.

Willughby, Francis. *Francis Willughby's Book of Games: A Seventeenth-century Treatise on Sports, Games, and Pastimes*. Ed. and introd. by David Cram, Jeffrey L. Forgeng and Dorothy Johnston. Aldershot: Ashgate, 2003.

Wood, Frances. *The Silk Road: Two Thousand Years in the Heart of Asia*. London: Folio Society, 2002.

Yolom, Marilyn. *Birth of the Chess Queen: A History*. New York: Harper Collins, 2004.

Yu, Ivan. *Interview*. 2006.

Zanazzo, Luigi. *Canti popolari romani [raccolti da] Giggi Zanazzo: con un saggio di canti del Lazio e Uno studio sulle melodie romane, con note musicali di Alessandro Parisotti*. Torino: S.T.E.N., 1910.

PRINTED IN ITALY
BY EDIZIONI POLISTAMPA
FLORENCE
2014